Lektürehilfen
William Shakespeare
»Macbeth«

Barron's Book Notes
Ernst Klett Verlag
Stuttgart Düsseldorf Leipzig

Reihe: Lektürehilfen Englisch
Verfasser dieses Bandes: Robert Owens Scott

Gedruckt auf Recyclingpapier,
hergestellt aus 100% Altpapier

Die Deutsche Bibliothek – CIP-Einheitsaufnahme

Scott, Robert Owens:
Lektürehilfen William Shakespeare, „Macbeth" /
[Verf. dieses Bd.: Robert Owens Scott]. – 7. Aufl. –
Stuttgart; Düsseldorf; Leipzig: Klett, 1998
(Reihe: Lektürehilfen Englisch) (Barron's book notes)
ISBN 3-12-922223-5

Abbildung auf dem Umschlag: Frontispiece of the First Folio edition 1623,
the Droeshout engraving (Ausschnitt)

Internetadresse: http://www.klett.de
7. Auflage 1998

Druck: Wilhelm Röck, Weinsberg
Einbandgestaltung: Bayerl & Ost, Frankfurt
ISBN 3-12-922223-5

CONTENTS

HOW TO USE THIS BOOK

You have to know how to approach literature in order to get the most out of it. This *Barron's Book Notes* volume follows a plan based on methods used by some of the best students to read a work of literature.

Begin with the guide's section on the author's life and times. As you read, try to form a clear picture of the author's personality, circumstances, and motives for writing the work. This background usually will make it easier for you to hear the author's tone of voice, and follow where the author is heading.

Then go over the rest of the introductory material—such sections as those on the plot, characters, setting, themes, and style of the work. Underline, or write down in your notebook, particular things to watch for, such as contrasts between characters and repeated literary devices. At this point, you may want to develop a system of symbols to use in marking your text as you read. (Of course, you should only mark up a book you own, not one that belongs to another person or a school.) Perhaps you will want to use a different letter for each character's name, a different number for each major theme of the book, a different color for each important symbol or literary device. Be prepared to mark up the pages of your book as you read. Put your marks in the margins so you can find them again easily.

Now comes the moment you've been waiting for—the time to start reading the work of literature. You may want to put aside your *Barron's Book Notes* volume until you've read the work all the way through. Or you may want to alternate, reading the *Book Notes* analysis of each section as soon as you have finished reading the corresponding part of the original. Before you move on, reread crucial passages you don't fully understand. (Don't take this guide's analysis for granted—make up your own mind as to what the work means.)

Once you've finished the whole work of literature, you may want to review it right away, so you can firm up your ideas about what it means. You may want to leaf through the book concentrating on passages you marked in reference to one character or one theme. This is also a good time to reread the *Book Notes* introductory material, which pulls together insights on specific topics.

When it comes time to prepare for a test or to write a paper, you'll already have formed ideas about the work. You'll be able to go back through it, refreshing your memory as to the author's exact words and perspective, so that you can support your opinions with evidence drawn straight from the work. Patterns will emerge, and ideas will fall into place; your essay question or term paper will almost write itself. Give yourself a dry run with one of the sample tests in the guide. These tests present both multiple-choice and essay questions. An accompanying section gives answers to the multiple-choice questions as well as suggestions for writing the essays. If you have to select a term paper topic, you may choose one from the list of suggestions in this book. This guide also provides you with a reading list, to help you when you start research for a term paper, and a selection of provocative comments by critics, to spark your thinking before you write.

THE AUTHOR AND HIS TIMES

Macbeth was first performed in 1606, three years after James I succeeded Elizabeth I on the English throne. By that time, William Shakespeare was the most popular playwright in England, and his company, which had been called the Chamberlain's Men under Queen Elizabeth, was renamed the King's Men.

You can see from the subject and content of *Macbeth* that Shakespeare was writing to please the new king. At the time James became James I of England, he was already James VI of Scotland, so a play like Macbeth about Scottish history was a tribute to him. This play was especially flattering because James was of the Stuart line of kings, and supposedly the Stuarts were descended from Banquo, who appears in the play as a brave, noble, honest man. Also, James wrote a book called *Demonology*, and he would have been very interested in the scenes with the witches.

It is not unusual that Shakespeare would have written *Macbeth* with an eye toward gratifying his patron. Shakespeare was a commercial playwright—he wrote and produced plays to sell tickets and make money.

One of his early plays—*Titus Andronicus*—was popular for the same reason certain movies sell a lot of tickets today: it is full of blood and gore. The witches and the battles of *Macbeth*, too, may have been there in part to appeal to the audience.

It was Shakespeare's financial success as a playwright that restored his family's sagging fortunes. John Shakespeare, William's father, was the son of a farmer. He opened a shop in Stratford-upon-Avon and eventually become one of the town's leading citizens.

John married Mary Arden, the daughter of his father's landlord. Mary was a gentle, cultivated woman, and their marriage helped John socially in Stratford.

William, their first son, was born in 1564. It seems that by the time he was twenty his father was deeply in debt, and John's name disappeared from the list of town councillors. Years later, when William was financially well off, he bought his father a coat of arms, which let John sign himself as an official "gentleman."

So Shakespeare was no aristocrat who wrote plays as an intellectual pursuit. He was a craftsman who earned his living as a dramatist.

We don't know much about Shakespeare's life. When he was eighteen, he married Anne Hathaway, who was twenty-six. They had three children, two girls and a boy, and the boy, Hamnet, died young. By his mid-twenties, Shakespeare was a successful actor and playwright in London, and he stayed in the theater until he died, in 1616.

Macbeth was written relatively late in Shakespeare's career—when he was in his forties. It was the last of what are considered the four great tragedies. (The others are *Hamlet, Othello,* and *King Lear.*) *Macbeth* is one of the shortest of Shakespeare's works, and its economy is a sign that its author was a master of his craft. You are amazed at the playwright's keen understanding of human nature and his skill in expressing his insights through dramatic verse as, step by step, he makes the spiritual downfall of Macbeth, the title character, horrifyingly clear.

All Shakespeare's plays seem to brim over with ideas—he is always juggling several possibilities about life. England, too, was in the midst of a highly interesting period, full of change.

Queen Elizabeth was a great queen, and under her rule England had won a war against Spain, which established it as a world power. America was being explored. Old ideas about government and law were changing. London was becoming a fabulous city, filling with people from the countryside. Even the English language was changing, as people from distant areas came together and added new words and expressions to the common language.

More than a half-century earlier, Henry VIII, Elizabeth's father, had broken away from the Roman Catholic Church and established the Church of England. Forty years later, in the middle of the 17th century, King Charles I would lose his head, executed by the Puritans in a civil war.

Elizabeth was not as secure on the throne as you might think. Though her grandfather, Henry VII, had stripped the nobles of England of much power, Elizabeth still struggled with them throughout her reign. She had to be a political genius to play them against each other, to avoid the plottings of the Roman Catholics and to overcome the country's financial mess created by her father, Henry VIII.

A lot was "modern," a lot was "medieval" about the way people thought in Shakespeare's time. People were superstitious, and the superstitions became mixed up with religion. Things that nobody understood were often attributed to supernatural forces.

You can feel some of these things moving behind the scenes as you read *Macbeth*. But none of this background—not the influence of James I or the intrigues of Elizabeth's court or the superstitions of the times—should determine the way you read the play. It has a life of its own, breathed into it by Shakespeare's talent and art. It stands on its own and must be evaluated on its own terms. So now let's turn to the play itself.

THE PLAY

The Plot

On a deserted field, with lightning and thunder overhead, we see three eerie witches. They chant spells, make plans to meet someone named Macbeth, and vanish into thin air.

In a military camp not far away are King Duncan of Scotland and some of his followers. A battle is raging nearby. We learn there is a rebellion against the King. He is too old to fight himself, and wants to know how his army is doing.

A badly wounded soldier reports that the battle was horribly bloody but the brave Thane of Glamis, Macbeth, saved the day, fighting fearlessly and killing the rebels' leader. (Thanes were Scottish noblemen.) Duncan is moved by Macbeth's courage.

The Thane of Ross arrives with more news: the Thane of Cawdor, one of Duncan's trusted captains, is a traitor. When Duncan learns that his army has won, he orders the Thane of Cawdor executed and indicates that Macbeth inherit his title.

Before Duncan's men can reach Macbeth to tell him the good news, Macbeth and Banquo, who have led Duncan's army together, come upon the three witches. Banquo thinks the three weird women are bizarre and funny, but Macbeth is strangely fascinated by them. They greet Macbeth with two predictions: that he will be Thane of Cawdor and that he will be king. Then they prophesy that though Banquo will never be a king, his children will be kings. And then the witches vanish.

Macbeth and Banquo cannot believe their eyes. As they joke uneasily about the predictions, they are interrupted by Duncan's messengers, who announce that Macbeth is now Thane of Cawdor. Suddenly, the witches are no laughing matter. Macbeth's mind is racing. Could he actually become king someday?

King Duncan personally thanks Macbeth for his bravery in the following scene, at his palace. But at the same time Duncan announces that his son Malcolm will inherit the throne. That is not good news for Macbeth. You can see already that he wants to wear the crown himself.

At Macbeth's castle, Lady Macbeth reads a letter from her husband telling her about the witches. It is clear that she will be willing to do anything to see Macbeth king. When the news arrives that Duncan will spend the night at her castle, she's amazed at his stupidity—or his innocence—and thrilled to have the chance to murder him.

That night, as the royal party is being entertained, Duncan's hosts secretly plot his death. Macbeth is scared of what he is about to do, and wants to back out, but his wife makes it clear that if he doesn't kill Duncan, she won't consider him a man. Macbeth commits the murder, but he is appalled by his deed.

When the King's body is discovered the next morning, nobody seems more shocked or surprised than Macbeth and his Lady. Macbeth blames Duncan's servants and kills them—pretending he is so enraged he cannot stop himself. Duncan's sons, Malcolm and Donalbain, sense treason and treachery and decide to run away, afraid that they will be killed, too. Macbeth has himself crowned king. The witches' predictions have come true, and Macbeth seems to have all he wants.

But Macbeth is not happy. He's afraid that some of the thanes suspect Duncan was not really killed by his servants. Worse, Macbeth's friend Banquo was told by the witches that he would father kings. To prevent that, Macbeth decides, he must also murder Banquo. This time without Lady Macbeth's help, Macbeth sends three men to kill Banquo and his son, Fleance. Banquo's throat is slit, but Fleance manages to escape.

On the night of his friend's murder Macbeth holds a great feast. But the merrymaking is spoiled by the appearance of Banquo's ghost. Macbeth is the only person there who can see him, and it makes him rave like a madman.

Terrified now of losing the crown, Macbeth goes back to the witches. They tell him three things: first, that he should fear Macduff, the Thane of Fife; second, that Macbeth will never be harmed by any man born of woman; and third, that he will never be defeated until Birnam Wood moves to Dunsinane Hill. Two out of three of the predictions sound comforting, but the witches go on to show Macbeth a vision of Banquo as father to a line of kings. The vision makes Macbeth furious, but the predictions make him even more ruthless.

Macbeth soon learns that the witches gave him good advice about fearing Macduff. The Thane of Fife has gone to England to meet with Malcolm, the rightful king, and plan a revolt. In his rage, Macbeth has Macduff's wife and children murdered.

When Macduff hears the news, his grief makes him even more determined to overthrow the tyrant Macbeth. He and Malcolm set out from England with ten thousand men.

In Scotland, Macbeth's world is falling apart. His followers are deserting him; his wife has lost her mind. Only his pride and his confidence in the witches' predictions keep him going.

As Malcolm is approaching Macbeth's castle at Dunsinane, he orders his troops to cut branches from trees in nearby Birnam Wood and carry them as disguises.

Macbeth at Dunsinane is waiting for the attackers when he's told that his wife is dead; she has killed herself. He barely has time to react before a report arrives that Birnam Wood seems to be *moving*—toward the castle! Furious, frightened, and desperate, Macbeth calls out his troops.

Malcolm's army throw down the branches and the battle begins. Macbeth's men hardly put up a fight, but Macbeth battles like a trapped animal.

Finally, Macbeth comes face to face with Macduff, who has been looking for him in the battlefield. Macbeth warns his enemy that no man born of woman can harm him. Macduff isn't frightened—he was "untimely ripped" from his mother's womb. (Today we would call it a cesarean section.) Though he knows the end has come, Macbeth fights on and is killed.

In triumph, Macduff carries Macbeth's severed head out to the people, who turn to Malcolm as their rightful king.

The Characters

Macbeth

Macbeth is a character of powerful contradictions. He is a man who, for the sake of his ambition, is willing to murder his king and his best friend. At the same time, he has a conscience that is so strong that just the thought of his crimes torments him. In fact, even before he commits his crimes the thought of them makes him miserable.

Is Macbeth a horrible monster or is he a sensitive man—a victim of witches and his own ambitions? Or is he both? If he is both, how can the two sides of his nature exist side by side?

To answer those questions, let's first look at what he does. Then we will look at how he feels about what he does. In the play, of course, the two go together.

His actions *are* monstrous. If Macbeth were a criminal brought to trial, the list of the charges against him would be long:

1. He murders his king, who is also a relative. The crime is treasonous and sacrilegious, since every king is set on his throne by God. Macbeth's guilt is even blacker because the King was his guest at the time of the murder. A host has responsibility to protect his guest.

2. He hires men to kill his best friend, Banquo. He wants the men to kill Banquo's young son, Fleance, too, but Fleance escapes.

3. He sends men to kill Macduff's wife and children.

4. Having taken the crown by murder, he keeps it by deception. He plants spies in all the nobles' homes and spreads lies about Malcolm, who should rightfully inherit the throne.

5. More crimes are referred to but not specified. Macbeth rules by terror, since he does not deserve—or have—anybody's loyalty. Describing Scotland under Macbeth's rule, Macduff says, "Each new morn / New widows howl, new orphans cry, new sorrows / Strike heaven on the face . . ." (*Act IV, Scene iii, lines 4–6*).

So Macbeth does horrible things, but that is not the whole story. Macbeth is different from some of Shakespeare's other villains like Iago (in *Othello*) and Richard III. The latter enjoy doing evil; they have renounced what we think of as normal ethics and morality. Macbeth's feelings are more complicated. In the beginning of the play, at least, he appears to have a conscience that tells him what he's doing is wrong. Or is he just afraid of the consequences of his actions?

He is never able to enjoy the crown he has taken. He experiences nothing but anguish. Is that simply because he is afraid of losing the crown, or is his conscience bothering him?

None of these questions is answered directly in the play. Each reader has to form his or her own opinion, based on the text.

Let's look at how Macbeth feels about each of the crimes we listed before:

1. Killing Duncan horrifies Macbeth. Before the murder, he tries to tell Lady Macbeth that he will not go through with it. She has to goad him into killing the King. After committing the murder, Macbeth seems almost delirious. He says that ". . . all great Neptune's ocean [will not] wash this blood / Clean from my hand" (*Act II, Scene ii, lines 60–61*).

2. When he murders Banquo, Macbeth is still in torment, but the cause of his anguish seems to have changed. He is afraid of Banquo, because Banquo knows about the witches and because the witches predicted that his descendents would be kings. Banquo's death, he says, will put his mind at rest.

3. We are never told how Macbeth feels about the murder of Macduff's wife and children. Their killing gains him nothing. He has good reason to fear Macduff, but slaughtering his enemy's family is pointless.

Macbeth seems to order their murder for spite, out of a feeling of desperation. Despite the witches' new prophesies, which appear to be reassuring, he is afraid of losing the crown. Since he cannot get at Macduff directly, he lets loose this senseless violence.

4. The spies Macbeth plants show how desperate and paranoid he is. He sees enemies—real or imagined—everywhere.

5. The other unspecified acts of violence serve no purpose, as far as we can see, beyond terrifying his subjects so much they won't resist him. Macbeth is striking out at random, and his moral sense seems to have entirely disappeared. The brave hero we met in Act I, who at least *seemed* honorable, is completely twisted.

You can see how much his crimes have cost Macbeth. His reaction to Lady Macbeth's death is a sign of complete despair—all feeling is dead in him. His famous speech upon hearing of her suicide—"To-morrow, and tomorrow, and tomorrow . . ." (*Act V, Scene v, lines 17–28*)—is less an expression of grief than it is a speech about the utter meaninglessness of life.

You wonder how all this has happened. If he was so horrified by first the idea and then the fact of Duncan's murder, why did he do it? And why commit the other crimes?

Apparently his ambition is stronger than his conscience. The witches tempt him with the idea of becoming king. Lady Macbeth helps him overcome his natural hesitation to commit murder. But Macbeth himself chooses between his honor and the crown—and between salvation in the next world and material gain in this one.

Once he has killed to get the crown, the other crimes seem inevitable. In order to keep what he has taken, Macbeth learns to lie and kill as a matter of course. His values become totally confused. "Fair is foul, and foul is fair" to him now; he has lost track of the difference.

All that seems left in the end is his pride. You respect him when he fights to the death rather than be displayed as the monster he is. But some people think that if Macbeth had not been so proud he would not have wanted to be king to begin with, and that if he had been humbler he would have repented.

Another aspect of Macbeth is his active imagination. Considering Duncan's murder, he can vividly picture all the possible consequences. His imagination pursues him throughout the play. He's continually reliving his crimes and fantasizing about present and future dangers. Nothing Lady Macbeth can say will quiet his mind.

At times he seems crazy—or haunted.

Before he kills Duncan, Macbeth sees a dagger floating in the air. After the murder, he hears voices. And later he sees Banquo's ghost. You are never quite sure if these are hallucinations—the imaginings of a sick mind—or if they are apparitions, like the witches. You begin to wonder how real *they* are.

Lady Macbeth

At the beginning of the play Lady Macbeth, unlike her husband, seems to have only one opinion about murder: if it helps her to get what she wants, she is in favor of it. For the first two acts of the play, some readers think she is the most interesting character. Their fascination is probably based on her total lack of scruples.

Lady Macbeth is a strong woman. She is a twisted example of the saying, "Behind every great man there's a woman." Once she sees that her husband's ambition has been inflamed, she is willing to risk anything to help him get the crown.

She understands her husband very well:

> Yet do I fear thy nature;
> It is too full o' th' milk of human kindness
> To catch the nearest way.
> (*Act I, Scene v, lines 17–19*)

In other words, she knows that Macbeth's conscience will stand in the way of his ambition.

For the sake of their "prize," she renounces all the soft, human parts of her own nature. In a play so full of supernatural events, we can take her literally if we want to when she calls upon ". . . spirits / That tend on mortal thoughts . . ." to "Stop up th' access and passage to remorse / That no compunctious visitings of nature / Shake my fell purpose . . ." (*Act I, Scene v, lines 41–42* and *45–47*).

It is as if she were tearing her heart out to make her husband king.

Lady Macbeth's singleness of purpose seems to prove that she has been successful in emptying herself of human feeling. When Macbeth tries to back out of committing the murder, she treats him with contempt. She questions his manhood and shames him into doing it.

Look at how effortlessly she lies. When Duncan, whom she plans to kill, arrives at the castle, her welcoming speech drips with false graciousness. While Macbeth has horrifying visions, Lady Macbeth seems cool and literal minded. To her, Duncan's blood is just something to be washed off her hands. Worrying over things you cannot alter is a waste of time, she says.

But Lady Macbeth is not as simple as she seems. By the end of the play she has killed herself to escape the horrible nightmares that torment her. Shakespeare seems to be saying that guilt and fear can be suppressed for a time, but they cannot be done away with entirely.

Some readers find Lady Macbeth a fascinating portrait of a horrible murderer. They see her actions as frighteningly amoral, and her madness and death as divine justice. Others see Lady Macbeth as a tragic figure. They are awed by her strength, her determination, and her resourcefulness. To them, the tragedy is that she wastes such qualities on evil deeds. And by the end, when her mind is rotten with madness, they can say she has struggled with her guilt every bit as much as her husband has with his.

Banquo

We can learn a lot about Macbeth by looking at Banquo. Banquo is a man of integrity. He is brave in battle but cautious in his actions. It is valuable to look at how he and Macbeth react differently to similar circumstances.

At the beginning of the play, they are equals. Macbeth and Banquo are leading Duncan's army—they fight side by side. They seem to be equally brave in combat.

Banquo and Macbeth meet the witches together, and Banquo's response to the prophesies is wiser than Macbeth's. He is skeptical from the beginning. When the witches first appear, he taunts them: "Speak then to me, who neither beg nor fear / Your favors nor your hate." (*Act I, Scene iii, lines 61–62*). After the prediction that Macbeth will become Thane of Cawdor comes true, Banquo is more cautious. He warns his friend not to be won over by small truths only to be betrayed in more important matters. He senses the women are evil, and he expects a trick.

Banquo has an honest and trusting nature. It never occurs to him that Macbeth may want to kill Duncan to make the prophesy come true. Later, even when he suspects that Macbeth killed the old King, Banquo does not suspect that he himself is in any danger.

It is interesting to note that Banquo does have some interest in the things the "weird sisters" promise him. He tells Macbeth that he dreamed about them. He also wonders if, since their prophesy for Macbeth came true, he should hope that his descendents will be kings.

But Banquo refuses to compromise his honor and his integrity to get the things he wants. He is willing to wait for the fullness of time to bring about whatever is coming. Also notice that Banquo, unlike Macbeth, does not hide the fact that he sometimes thinks about the three witches.

So it seems that Shakespeare formed Banquo's character the way he did to show how a man of honor would respond to the kind of temptation that Macbeth gives in to. There is probably another reason why Banquo is portrayed as he is. Historically, Banquo was an ancestor of King James I of England. *Macbeth* was first presented for James. In Holinshed's *Chronicles,* which was Shakespeare's source for the story, Banquo helped Macbeth murder the king. Many critics believe that Shakespeare changed Banquo's role to please King James.

The Witches

The three witches that Macbeth and Banquo meet are also called the "weird sisters." In Old English *wyrd* meant "fate." And it is part of their role in the play to act as the forces of fate.

But "fate" in what sense? Do they cause Macbeth's actions? What powers do they have, and what are the limits of their powers? In other words, do they *dictate* what will happen?

They certainly know things that no mortal could know. Even a person who knew that the Thane of Cawdor was a traitor would be awfully shrewd to guess that Macbeth would be given his title. And who without supernatural powers could have known that Macbeth would only be defeated when Birnam Wood moved to Dunsinane?

The witches have other supernatural powers. They can cause storms, and they appear and disappear at will.

But their powers are limited. Look at Act I, Scene iii. The First Witch has been insulted by a sailor's wife. When the witch asked the woman for a chestnut, the woman says, "Aroint thee, witch!" In other words, "Get lost!" The witch doesn't seem to be able to harm the woman directly. Instead, she sends a storm to disturb the sailor's ship. Even at that, her powers are limited: ". . . his bark cannot be lost . . .", the witch says.

These hags lead Macbeth on to destroy himself. Their predictions are temptations. They never lie, they never tell Macbeth he has to *do* anything, they just give the trick answers. In that sense they are agents of the devil, out for his soul; they trick him into damning himself.

But it is clear that the responsibility for the crimes is Macbeth's. Nothing the witches did forced him to commit them. He was wrong to hear their words as an invitation to murder the King. Still, you wonder if Macbeth would have murdered anybody if he had not met the witches. And you can argue that either way.

Malcolm

Malcolm represents the rightful order that Macbeth disturbs. Duncan, who is a good and wise king, names his son the Prince of Cumberland and heir to the throne.

Will Malcolm make a good king? Clearly, Shakespeare wants us to believe he will. Though Malcolm is young, he is already wise. He and his brother Donalbain are smart enough to get away from Macbeth's castle as soon as possible after their father's murder. After safely reaching England, Malcolm does not rashly try to reclaim the throne. Instead, he waits until the time is right.

In his scene with Macduff, Malcolm displays cleverness and verbal skill. He manipulates Macduff, testing his loyalty, but he does it only for the good of his people and his country.

In the final speech of the play, Malcolm demonstrates his fitness for kingship. Macbeth has been killed, and Malcolm is about to be crowned. Like his father, in Act I, Malcolm's first concern is to reward those who have helped him. The speech is full of images of divine grace and natural order.

Duncan

The King makes his final exit before the end of Act I, and he is murdered offstage early in Act II. Not having a lot of time to develop Duncan's character, Shakespeare works in broad, clear strokes.

Duncan is "a most sainted king" (*Act IV, Scene iii, line 109*), as Macduff calls him. His murder is a crime that has no justification. Even Macbeth calls him "the gracious Duncan" (*Act III, Scene i, line 66*).

We know that Duncan is old—otherwise he would be in combat with his army. Owing to his age, he has to anxiously await word from the field.

His generosity is clearly demonstrated by the way he treats Macbeth. He rewards the noble Macbeth immediately after hearing about his bravery.

Duncan is also gracious to Lady Macbeth. Even though he is actually honoring Macbeth and his wife by spending the night at their castle, he behaves as if they were doing him a favor.

The person who best sums up Duncan's nature is his murderer—Macbeth: ". . . this Duncan / Hath borne his faculties so meek, hath been / So clear in his great office, that his virtues / Will plead like angels . . ." (*Act I, Scene vii, lines 16–19*).

Macduff

Macduff is Macbeth's major adversary. Malcolm is the rightful king and leads the forces to overthrow the tyrant, but Macduff is a thorn in Macbeth's side from the beginning. In the end, he kills Macbeth.

Until the murder of his wife and children, Macduff has not been hurt personally by Macbeth. He opposes Macbeth because he knows right from wrong. He never wants the crown for himself. His desire is to see the rightful king on the throne.

He refuses to play games. He will not attend Macbeth's crowning or put in an appearance at the tyrant's feast just to keep up appearances.

Macduff is not clever with words. He voices his disapproval of Macbeth not by statements but by his absence. Macduff's simple honesty is revealed when he is tested by Malcolm in Act IV, Scene iii. In a play like *Macbeth,* in which many people and things are not what they appear to be, Macduff is like a breath of fresh air.

Maturity is another trait of Macduff's. He takes the news of his wife and children's murder like a blow squarely on the chin. By having the courage to feel his grief, he is able to convert his pain into a burning desire for righteous revenge.

Other Elements

SETTING

The settings of Shakespeare's plays generally come more from the dramatic needs of the story than from any literal sense of the place. *Macbeth* is no exception.

Most of the action takes place in Scotland. There are at least two reasons: 1. Shakespeare invented the plot of *Macbeth* by combining several stories out of Scottish history he found in Holinshed's *Chronicles;* and 2. James I, who was King of England when the play was written, was a Scot. But reading books about the Scottish landscape will not help you understand the setting of *Macbeth.* Instead, read the play.

The Scotland of *Macbeth* seems rough and somewhat primitive. Each thane has his castle, and in between there are woods and fields. None of the action takes place in anything like a city.

The play has a murky feeling, which is reflected in the setting. The action starts in the open fields, but the air is clouded by the smoke of battle. Lightning and thunder fill the sky. Most of the scenes in Macbeth's castle take place at night. Torches are needed to see anything at all.

THEMES

Here are some of the major themes in *Macbeth.* Notice that each is expressed through some combination of plot, character, and language.

1. AN ANATOMY OF EVIL

A powerful sense of evil hangs over every scene in the play. Each character has to either fight or give in to it. The play makes several points about the nature of evil. The first point is that evil is contrary to human nature. Macbeth and Lady Macbeth have to contort their natures to murder Duncan. First, Lady Macbeth has to beg evil spirits to tear all human feeling from her, and then she has to make her husband ignore his own conscience. But the play also says that human nature cannot be avoided indefinitely. By the end of the play, both characters have been destroyed from within. Fear and guilt drive Lady Macbeth mad; Macbeth sees life as an empty, meaningless charade.

The second point is that it is evil to disrupt the natural order of the world. In nature, everything happens in its own time. A flower blooms when the laws of nature say it should, neither sooner nor later. When Macbeth takes the crown by murder, he upsets the natural order of his life—*and* the order of Scotland. Without the rightful, God-given king on the throne all society is disordered; under a usurper there can only be evil and chaos. Even nature becomes upset: it's dark during the day; horses eat each other; owls kill falcons. Nearly every scene has references to unnatural deeds or occurrences. When Macbeth is killed and Malcolm takes the throne, the natural order is restored.

The third point is that evil is a disease. Like a disease, evil infects its victims and makes them sicken until they die. Once Macbeth kills Duncan, he is committed to a course of lying and killing. His sense of right and wrong is eaten away. Even before he is killed, Macbeth is dying of a diseased spirit. Scotland is also infected, and Macbeth is its disease. The longer he is king, the worse things get. When Macbeth is overthrown, the country is healed.

2. AMBITION

Many readers feel that Macbeth's downfall is caused by his ambition. At the beginning of the play, Macbeth seems to be a brave, noble, and loyal thane.

For his desire to become king, he is willing to turn his back on what he knows to be right. Lady Macbeth, because of her ambition for her husband, uses all her strength and intelligence for evil purposes. They are very unlike Banquo, who will not compromise his honor for anything.

3. APPEARANCE VERSUS REALITY

Practically nothing in the play is what it appears to be. The witches' predictions sound like good news; actually, they lead to death and destruction. Macbeth and his wife seem like gracious hosts; actually, they are plotting murder. The Macbeths appear to achieve their heart's desires; in reality, they only gain torment and death. In reading the play, examine each scene to compare what appears to be happening with what is really happening.

4. HONOR AND LOYALTY

In a feudal society such as the one in *Macbeth,* peace and order are maintained largely through honor and loyalty. Men of honor obey certain rules. Macbeth throws all ideas of honor out the window. Once he has done that, the country is in turmoil. Nobody knows whom he can trust. Look at what Macduff has to go through to win Malcolm's trust in Act IV. In Act V, it is made very clear that the few followers Macbeth has left have been forced to stay with him. They feel no sense of loyalty toward him. When it comes time to fight, they just give up.

5. FATE AND DESTINY

The play suggests that a person should trust his destiny to a higher power. After encountering the three witches, Macbeth tries to take fate into his own hands, and that action brings him nothing but grief.

Malcolm, on the other hand, trusts that all things will work out ". . . by the grace of Grace [in other words, heaven]" (*Act V, Scene viii, line 72*). "Be what you're meant to be," the play seems to be saying.

SOURCES

The story of *Macbeth* is a combination of two stories found in Holinshed's *Chronicles of England, Scotland, and Ireland*. Shakespeare developed many of the plots and characters for his plays from this book of history and legend.

Holinshed tells one story about a man named Macbeth who killed a king named Duncan, but this story is different from the play in several important ways. The Duncan of the story was a bad king. He did not care about his people, and Banquo helped Macbeth overthrow him.

Shakespeare combined that story with another Holinshed story about someone named Donwald who killed a king named Duff. Duff was a good and pious king, and was Donwald's guest when he was murdered. Also, Donwald killed Duff because his wife urged him to.

For the supernatural elements of the play, Shakespeare might have consulted a book called *Demonology*, written by none other than King James I himself. (Remember that *Macbeth* was first presented at James' court.) In his book, James states that witches can predict the future.

POINT OF VIEW

Shakespeare takes a clear moral stance in telling the story of Macbeth. He portrays humans as creatures capable of good but in danger of giving in to the temptations of evil. Evil is introduced through supernatural beings—the witches. You could say Macbeth is as much a victim of their deception and his own ambition as he is a victimizer of others.

All evildoers are punished. The numerous mentions of heaven and hell remind us that good people who are killed will find eternal happiness, while those who do evil will suffer eternal damnation.

It is important not to confuse the point of view that Shakespeare gives to a character with the playwright's own point of view. For example, Macbeth's "tomorrow and tomorrow" speech says that life is meaningless, but the play as a whole says just the opposite. Macbeth's utter despair at that moment is a result of his evil deeds. The very fact that he and Lady Macbeth are punished for their wickedness is proof of a higher good which gives meaning to life.

FORM AND STRUCTURE

Like all of Shakespeare's plays, *Macbeth* is divided into five acts. Each act is broken down further into scenes. Editors disagree about the proper division of scenes in Act V. Some divide it into six scenes. Others make eight scenes from the same text, as we have in the scene-by-scene analysis, and still others make it into nine scenes. All these versions have the same text; only the divisions are different.

Let's look at the form of the play in terms of storytelling. At each moment in the play, there is a question that keeps our interest. That is called dramatic tension.

From the point when Macbeth hears the witches' prophesies, he is obviously enticed by the idea of becoming king. We wonder what he will do about it.

Will he kill Duncan? Once the murder has been committed, we wonder what the consequences will be.

Macbeth becomes king, but some are suspicious. What will happen to Banquo and Macduff? In the next section of the play, Macbeth tries to make his position secure through murder. We can see that things are only getting worse for him, and we wonder how long he can hold on.

In Act IV, the end of the play is set up. Macbeth visits the witches, who give him new prophesies. Anybody who is following the story should suspect that they are deceiving him somehow, but we do not know how. In the same act, Malcolm and Macduff join together to defeat Macbeth. Now we wait for the final battle.

Notice how skillfully Shakespeare maintains suspense up to the end. Macbeth's followers have deserted him; Birnam Wood has come to Dunsinane. He seems doomed, but we know that he cannot be defeated by any man born of woman. Who can beat him, then? Finally, Macduff reveals his secret, and Macbeth is killed. All that remains is to cheer the new and rightful king, Malcolm.

ELIZABETHAN ENGLISH

All languages change. Differences in pronunciation and word choice are apparent even between parents and their children. If language differences can appear in one generation, it is only to be expected that the English used by Shakespeare four hundred years ago will diverge markedly from the English that is used today. The following information on Shakespeare's language will help you to a fuller understanding of *Macbeth*.

Changes in Word Classes

Adjectives, nouns, and verbs were less rigidly confined to particular classes in Shakespeare's day. For example, verbs were often used as nouns. In Act I, Scene vii, line 5, Macbeth uses *be* as a noun:

> . . . that but this blow
> Might be the be-all and the end-all . . .

And nouns could be used as verbs, as when *incarnadine,* which was a color, was used to mean "redden":

> Will all great Neptune's ocean wash this blood
> Clean from my hand? No; this my hand will rather
> The multitudinous seas incarnadine
> (*II, ii, 59–61*)

Adjectives could also be used as adverbs. In the above quotation *clean* is used in a position where contemporary usage would require a form like *entirely,* and *easy* is used for "easily" in:

> Let's not consort with them.
> To show an unfelt sorrow is an office
> Which the false man does easy.
> (*II, iii, 137–38*)

They could also be used as nouns, as in:

> If a man were porter of hell gate, he should have
> old turning the key.
> (*II, iii, 1–2*)

In this instance, *old* is the equivalent of "frequent opportunity."

Changes in Meanings of Words

The meanings of words undergo changes, a process that can be illustrated by the fact that *chip* extended its meaning from a small piece of wood to a small piece of silicon. Many of the words in Shakespeare's plays still exist today but their meanings have changed. The "astonishment" in:

> and when he reads
> Thy personal venture in the rebels' fight,
> His wonders and his praises do contend . . .
>
> *(I, iii, 90–92)*

Or, more fundamental, *earnest* meant "token of an agreement" *(I, iii, 104)*, *line* meant "strengthen" *(I, iii, 112)*, *missives* meant "messengers" *(I, v, 6)*, *illness* meant "wickedness" *(I, v, 20)*, and *sightless* meant "invisible":

> Wherever in your sightless substances
> You wait on nature's mischief!
>
> *(I, v, 50–51)*

Vocabulary Loss

Words not only change their meanings, but are frequently discarded from the language. In the past *leman* meant "sweetheart" and *sooth* meant "truth." The following words used in *Macbeth* are no longer current in English but their meaning can usually be gauged from the context in which they occur.

paddock *(I, i, 9)*: toad
masterdom *(I, v, 70)*: mastery
favour *(I, v, 72)*: countenance, face
jutty *(I, vi, 6)*: part of a building
in compt *(I, vi, 26)*: subject to account
trammel up *(I, vii, 3)*: entangle
afeard *(I, vii, 39)*: afraid
limbeck *(I, vii, 68)*: skull, container of the brain
dudgeon *(II, i, 46)*: handle
sleave *(II, ii, 36)*: silk thread, silk
goose *(II, iii, 15)*: smoothing iron
avouch *(III, i, 119)*: justify

ecstasy (*III, ii, 22*): fit
seeling (*III, ii, 46*): blinding
lated (*III, iii, 6*): belated
trenched (*III, iv, 26*): cut
flaws (*III, iv, 62*): sudden gusts
owe (*III, iv, 112*): own
drab (*IV, i, 31*): prostitute
sweaten (*IV, i, 65*): irregularly formed
gin (*IV, ii, 35*): snare
foisons (*IV, iii, 88*): abundant harvests
teems (*IV, iii, 176*): brings forth
mated (*V, i, 75*): confused

Verbs

Shakespearean verb forms differ from modern usage in these three main ways.

1. Questions and negatives could be formed without using *do/did*, as when Lady Macbeth asks "Know you not, he has?" (*I, vii, 30*). Today we would say, "Do you not know that he has?" Another instance occurs when Macbeth tells Banquo "I think not of them" (*II, i, 21*); modern usage demands, "I do not think of them."

Shakespeare had the option of using forms whereas contemporary usage permits the option of using the following two forms, whereas contemporary usage permits only the **a** forms:

a	**b**
Is the king going?	Goes the king?
Did the king go?	Went the king?
You do not look well	You look not well
You did not look well	You looked not well

2. A number of past participles and past-tense forms are used that would be ungrammatical today. Among these are: *forbid* for "forbidden," as in: "He shall live a man forbid" (*I, iii, 21*); *holp* for "helped," as in: "And his great love, sharp as his spur, hath holp him" (*I, v, 23*); *eat* for "ate," as in:

> 'Tis said they eat each other.
> They did so, to th' amazement of mine eyes"
> (*II, iv, 18*)

3. Archaic verb forms sometimes occur with *thou* and with *he/she/it:*

> As thou art in desire? Would'st thou have that
> Which thou esteem'st the ornament of life
> (*I, vii, 41–42*)

> Hath he asked for me?
> (*I, vii, 30*)

Pronouns

Shakespeare and his contemporaries had one extra pronoun—*thou*—which could be used in addressing a person who was one's equal or social inferior. *You* was obligatory if more than one person was addressed: "Stay you imperfect speakers, tell me more" (*I, iii, 70*), but it could also be used to indicate respect, as when Lady Macbeth told Duncan:

> Your servants ever
> Have theirs, themselves, and what is theirs, in compt.
> To make their audit at your Highness' pleasure,
> Still to return your own.
> (*I, vi, 25–28*)

Frequently, a person in power used *thou* to a child or a subordinate but was addressed *you* in return, as when Lady Macduff spoke to her son:

> *Lady Macduff:* Now, God help thee, poor monkey! But how wilt thou do for a father?

Son: If he were dead, you'd weep for him. If you would not, it were a good sign that I should quickly have a new father.

(*IV, ii, 57–61*)

But if *thou* was used inappropriately, it might be offensive. One of the witches uses *thou* in addressing Macbeth to underline the fact that Macbeth has, by his murders, reduced himself to their level:

Say if th' hadst rather hear it from our mouths,
Or from our masters?

(*IV, i, 62–63*)

One further pronominal reference warrants a comment. Duncan uses the royal plural *we* to stress the honor he is bestowing on Lady Macbeth by staying with her:

Fair and noble hostess,
We are your guest tonight.

(*I, vi, 24–25*)

But he uses *I* to stress his debt to Macbeth for winning the battle:

O worthiest cousin!
The sin of my ingratitude even now
Was heavy on me

(*I, iv, 14–16*)

Prepositions

Prepositions were less standardized in Elizabethan English than they are today, and so we find several uses in *Macbeth* that would have to be modified in contemporary speech. Among these are *on* for "to" in: "The victory fell on us" (*I, ii, 59*); *with* for "by" in: "Thence to be wrenched with an unlineal hand" (*III, i, 62*); *for* for "on account of" in: "For certain friends that are both his and mine" (*III, i, 120*); and *at . . . and* for "from . . . to" in:

> You know your own degrees; sit down:
> At first and last, the hearty welcome.
>
> (*III, iv, 1–2*)

Multiple Negation

Contemporary English requires only one negative per statement and regards such utterances as "I haven't none" as nonstandard. Shakespeare often used two or more negatives for emphasis, as when Macduff found the King dead:

> O horror, horror, horror! Tongue nor heart
> Cannot conceive nor name thee.
>
> (*II, iii, 66–67*)

And Macbeth says:

> Treason has done his worst: nor steel, nor
> poison,
> Malice domestic, foreign levy, nothing,
> Can touch him further.
>
> (*III, ii, 24–26*)

The Story

ACT I, SCENE I

Imagine that you are sitting in a theater waiting to see a play about a man named Macbeth. As the play begins lightning flashes, and instead of seeing this Macbeth, you see three weird-looking women. They must be witches; they are chanting spells. After making plans to meet Macbeth, they leave.

That's the whole scene—ten lines! Look at what Shakespeare accomplishes with this opening. By beginning the play with the witches instead of starting with Macbeth, he makes it clear that something wicked is going to happen. When we hear more about Macbeth and finally see him, we have to wonder why the three witches have business with him. So this scene establishes the mood of the play.

NOTE: Always read a scene in Shakespeare first to find out what happens and what the characters say to each other. Then read it again to see what you can learn not from *what* they say but *how* they say it. In other words, examine Shakespeare's use of language. For example: The witches say "Fair is foul, and foul is fair" (*line 10*). That line is like a riddle; it seems like nonsense but you can see it means something. Different versions of the same idea turn up all through the play. One thing the line is saying is that nothing in the play will be what it seems to be. And it is also letting you know, right away, that in Macbeth's Scotland everything is going to be confused and perverted.

ACT I, SCENE II

Lightning, thunder, and witches give way in this scene to blood, soldiers, and fighting. We still do not meet Macbeth, but we learn more about him.

What happens is simple: King Duncan, too old to fight, wants to know how his army is doing. A wounded soldier tells him. We learn that the Scottish soldiers are fighting two enemies at once: rebels from their own country and invaders from Norway.

The main thing we learn from this "bloody captain" is that Macbeth is a hero. The battle was awful, but Macbeth was fearless, fighting his way through the enemy and literally cutting the rebel leader in half. King Duncan is suitably impressed. We also hear for the first time about Macbeth's fellow-captain, Banquo, who is described as being just as brave as Macbeth.

The Thane of Ross arrives with a new report: the Thane of Cawdor is a traitor, but King Duncan's army has won. Duncan is upset that the Thane of Cawdor, whom he trusted, is a traitor. At the same time, he is very moved by Macbeth's bravery. He orders Cawdor's execution and rewards Macbeth by making him the new Thane of Cawdor. The Thanes of Ross and Angus leave to tell Macbeth.

NOTE: A lot of what you find out in this scene is "exposition"—information you have to have so you will know who people are and what has been happening before the play starts. Have you ever seen a play or movie in which somebody comes on and, for no apparent reason, starts telling who is who and what is going on? That is *bad* exposition. Look how skillfully Shakespeare gets his information across. By bringing on a bloody soldier, he dramatizes the offstage battle. Even without the words, you can tell how bad the fighting must have been. By keeping Duncan in the dark, Shakespeare justifies having the soldier give his report.

The theme of honor is introduced in this scene. Duncan says the bloody soldier's words and wounds both "smack of honor" (*line 45*). Macbeth is described as "brave" and "worthy," and he gets his reward. You can see that honor is very important to these people.

ACT I, SCENE III

In this scene we finally meet Macbeth. Macbeth encounters the witches, who tempt him with the idea of becoming king.

Lines 1–37

We learn more about the nature of the witches. They talk among themselves about the nasty things they have been doing. One has been passing the time killing swine (pigs), another has been plotting revenge on a sailor's wife who refused to give her a chestnut. Listening to them, we get the impression that a lot of bad things that happen to people and are called bad luck are actually caused by these hags.

Lines 37–87

Now we have heard that Macbeth is brave and worthy, but we also know that these evil creatures want to meet with him. We are ready to meet Macbeth himself, and in he comes with Banquo.

Look at the first thing he says: "So foul and fair a day I have not seen" (*line 37*). That sounds like what the witches said in Scene i! Is Shakespeare suggesting that Macbeth is not what he seems to be—a brave and loyal thane? You do not know yet, but you begin to wonder.

The witches predict what the future holds for Macbeth and Banquo. Macbeth, who is Thane of Glamis, will be Thane of Cawdor. That comes as a surprise to Macbeth, but not to us, of course. They also say he will be king one day. They tell Banquo he will be father to a line of kings, though he will never be one himself.

NOTE: We can learn something about Macbeth by studying the different ways he and Banquo respond to these predictions. Banquo asks Macbeth, "why do you start, and seem to fear / Things that do sound so fair?" (*lines 51–52*). Why indeed? Has he already been plotting to become king? Does he feel the witches have read his mind, and guessed how much he wants the crown? Or has his mind flashed ahead, wondering *how* this could possibly happen? Whatever, his reaction is that of a guilty man. Banquo, on the other hand, makes fun of the witches. He is curious about what they have to say, but that is all.

Lines 88–156

Ross and Angus arrive and tell Macbeth that he is now Thane of Cawdor. The witches told the truth! Look once again at the difference between Macbeth's response and Banquo's. Banquo is skeptical:

> And oftentimes, to win us to our harm,
> The instruments of darkness tell us truths,
> Win us with honest trifles, to betray's
> In deepest consequence.
>
> *Act I, Scene iii, lines 123–26*

He seems to be saying, "This could be a trick." Fair words can mean foul things.

Macbeth is already obsessed with the idea of being king. He knows Duncan would have to die first, and even though he says that the idea of murder "doth unfix my hair" (*line 135*), he's started to think about it.

From this point on, Macbeth is clearly hiding things. When Banquo comments that Macbeth is lost in thought, Macbeth lies to his friend, saying he was thinking about something else.

ACT I, SCENE IV

Lines 1–14

Duncan learns that the traitor Cawdor has been executed. It is important to note that he repented and asked for Duncan's forgiveness before he died. Through his honorable death, he seems to have made up for his sinful life.

Lines 15–59

Macbeth, Banquo, Ross, and Angus enter. In the exchange that follows, you can see Macbeth's desire to become king, even if the others can't.

The King greets Macbeth with genuine love and gratitude. In the presence of all the thanes, however, he names his son Malcolm the Prince of Cumberland. That means that Malcolm will inherit the throne when Duncan dies.

Macbeth responds to that announcement in an "aside," which means that he speaks his thoughts directly to the audience and it is understood that the other characters don't hear what he is saying. In his aside, Macbeth grumbles that Malcolm is now in his way. You begin to realize nothing will stop him.

NOTE: Notice the imagery of light and darkness in lines 15–52: "Stars, hide your fires; / Let not light see my black and deep desires." Throughout the play, light symbolizes good, and dark stands for evil. Macbeth has just taken one giant step toward evil.

ACT I, SCENE V

At Macbeth's castle, Lady Macbeth gets a letter from her husband telling her about the predictions. She dedicates herself to helping Macbeth become king. When she learns that Duncan will spend the night at their castle, she immediately decides to kill him.

Lady Macbeth tells us something vital about her husband—that, by nature, he is not ruthless. She says that even if he wants something so badly he feels like his life depends on it, he will not cheat to get it. She sees that as a flaw in his character!

Lady Macbeth does not have that problem. The woman's resolution is so intense it is frightening. Her speech in lines 39–55 is worth looking at, because it expresses her determination with some of the most potent imagery to be found anywhere in Shakespeare's plays. She actually asks spirits to "unsex" her and "take [her] milk for gall." And look how she picks up the light-dark imagery: "Come, thick night, / And pall thee in the dunnest smoke of hell." If Macbeth took a giant step toward evil, his wife makes a gigantic leap!

Notice how when Macbeth comes in, Lady Macbeth takes charge and starts talking about the murder right away. She doesn't even have to *ask* if he's considered it; she *knows* he has. She does most of the talking, and several times she tells him to leave everything to her. Macbeth does not agree to killing Duncan, but he does not refuse, either.

ACT I, SCENE VI

Duncan, his sons Malcolm and Donalbain, and Banquo and some other thanes arrive at Macbeth's castle. They comment on what a pleasant place it is. Lady Macbeth welcomes them warmly.

Here is a scene in which *nothing* is what it seems. Macbeth's castle is really a place of evil and death. The gracious hostess who delivers such pretty speeches is actually just waiting for the chance to murder her guest of honor.

NOTE: Shakespeare uses a technique in this scene called dramatic irony. We as readers know about the double meanings in the scene. Except for Lady Macbeth, the characters are not aware of them. The scene is more interesting for us, because we know more than the characters do. Depending upon the way the scene is played, the effect can be funny, scary, or both.

ACT I, SCENE VII

Lines 1–28

Macbeth starts this scene in a state of emotional turmoil. As Lady Macbeth predicted, he wants to be king but he's afraid to kill Duncan. Having a vivid imagination, he can picture all the consequences of the murder before he commits it.

Two things make Macbeth hesitate: the fact that the murder is morally wrong, and the fear that he'll be punished for his crime. It's hard to say which reason, if either, is stronger. Though Macbeth does not seem like a religious man, there is a lot of religious imagery in this speech, with references to "angels" and "deep damnation" (*lines 19–20*).

Lines 29–82

Macbeth tells his wife that he cannot go through with the murder. She works on him to change his mind.

Lady Macbeth's first ploy is to mock her husband. She implies that he is a coward and even questions his manhood. Using the fact that she is a woman, and his wife, she twists the idea of motherhood into a way to get at him further:

> I have given suck, and know
> How tender 'tis to love the babe that milks me:
> I would, while it was smiling in my face,
> Have plucked my nipple from his boneless gums,
> And dashed the brains out, had I so sworn as you
> Have done to this.
>
> *Act I, Scene vii, lines 54–59*

It is hard to argue with that kind of resolution. Macbeth gives in a little. Instead of refusing again, he asks "If we should fail?" (*line 59*).

Sensing she is about to win, Lady Macbeth coolly recites the details of their plan; while Duncan's servants are in a drunken sleep, Macbeth can kill the king and blame the servants.

Macbeth himself is chilled by his wife's hard attitude toward the murder, but he's also convinced. The scene and the act end on a note of resolution. Macbeth will kill Duncan.

ACT II

ACT II, SCENE I

In the first scene of Act II, Shakespeare builds up suspense before the murder.

Lines 1–9

Banquo and his son Fleance talk casually about the night. In their short exchange, we learn three things: 1. that it is late and Banquo is sleepy (and we know what will happen once everybody goes to sleep); 2. that Banquo has some strange uneasiness which makes him unwilling to go to sleep; and 3. that Banquo has a son (that fact will become important later).

Lines 10–30

Macbeth comes in and talks with Banquo. Notice how nervous Banquo is. When he hears somebody coming he calls for his sword, even though he should feel safe in his friend's castle.

Shakespeare again uses the technique of dramatic irony. Banquo gives Macbeth a ring that is a present from Duncan for Lady Macbeth. We know, as Banquo does not, that the king is giving a gift to his murderer. We can imagine how Macbeth feels when Banquo says he dreamed of witches, and we know Macbeth is lying when he claims, "I think not of them" (*line 21*).

The two friends move further apart in this scene. When Banquo mentions the three witches, he is confiding his private thoughts to his friend. Macbeth dodges Banquo's honest comments, and begins hinting around by talking with Banquo about some business that will "make honor" for Banquo (*line 26*). Banquo responds politely but cautiously, saying that whatever he can do for Macbeth with a clear conscience he will do.

Lines 31–64

After Banquo and Fleance leave, Macbeth sends his servant off to Lady Macbeth with a message about his nightcap drink. That is probably a secret signal that everybody has gone to bed.

Macbeth prepares to commit the murder. His speech here is called a soliloquy because he is alone on stage. When you read or hear a soliloquy, you can assume that the character is speaking his true thoughts. Since he is talking to himself, why should he lie?

As soon as Macbeth is alone he has a vision. He sees a dagger floating in the air in front of him. It melts through his fingers when he tries to grab it but it will not go away. Then suddenly, the dagger appears to be covered with blood. Has Macbeth lost his mind? Or could the dagger be as real as the witches? Is he hallucinating or has some devil sent it as a sign? You cannot tell; and neither can Macbeth. He does not know whether to trust his eyes or his reason: "Mine eyes are made the fools o'the' other senses, / Or else worth all the rest" (*lines 44–45*).

At line 47, Macbeth's rational will takes over. "There's no such thing," he says about the dagger, and he never mentions it again. The imagery in the rest of this soliloquy shows that Macbeth knows exactly what he is doing. He says that "nature seems dead" (*line 50*). He mentions witchcraft and ghosts.

NOTE: *Unnatural* means "perverted," and in *Macbeth* the word works in many ways. In Shakespeare's time, people thought in terms of God's plan for mankind. This grand design was the "natural" order of the world. The devil was always trying to mess it up by tempting people to sin. So evil was "unnatural"; it corrupted the people God wanted to be good.

You will see the image of "unnaturalness" multiply around Macbeth as he mutilates his soul—or you might say his human nature. And since he's the king, the country reflects his spiritual sickness. It, too, becomes mutilated. Also notice as you read how the unnatural acts are reflected in nature—in animals and weather, for instance.

ACT II, SCENE II

In this scene, the murder takes place. Macbeth is nearly driven mad by the horror of what he's done. Lady Macbeth urges him to be practical: after all, there is no going back. They have killed their king.

NOTE: It is interesting that Shakespeare chooses to have Macbeth kill Duncan offstage. We can only guess why he wrote the scene that way, but here are two possible reasons: 1. Shakespeare wanted to focus not on the murder but on Macbeth's reaction to it; and 2. the bloody details supplied by our imaginations will be much worse than anything that could be done onstage.

Lines 1–13

Lady Macbeth waits alone while her husband kills Duncan. She seems excited by the idea of murder and pleased with herself because of her part in the plan.

Yet we also get a peek at her softer side. She says that she would have killed Duncan herself, but the old man looked too much like her father. This small reminder of Lady Macbeth's humanity will be important to our understanding of what happens to her at the end of the play.

Lines 13–56

Macbeth enters, his hands covered with Duncan's blood. Notice how the sharp, quick exchange of words between Macbeth and Lady Macbeth underscores the tension:

Lady: Did you not speak?
Macbeth: When?
Lady: Now.
Macbeth: As I descended?
Lady: Ay.

Act II, Scene ii, lines 16–17

As the scene proceeds, Macbeth and his wife behave in a manner exactly opposite from what we would expect. According to conventional logic, Macbeth, who is a soldier and has already killed many men in battle that day, should not be bothered by the murder. On the other hand, we would understand perfectly if his wife were upset by having been involved in a killing.

Look at what actually happens: Macbeth is horrified by what he has done. He says he has "hangman's hands" (*line 27*), and he is afraid that after having committed such a horrible deed he will never sleep again. Lady Macbeth is practical. She gives the advice you would expect to come from a soldier: "These deeds must not be thought / After these ways; so, it will make us mad" (*lines 32–33*).

When Lady Macbeth tells her husband to take the daggers he used for the murder back into Duncan's room, he refuses. She makes fun of him and takes them up herself.

We can understand the torture Macbeth is going through by realizing that he seems to consider the murder one of the most evil deeds ever committed. We would have to call this statement exaggeration:

> Will all great Neptune's ocean wash this blood
> Clean from my hand? No; this my hand will
>   rather
> The multitudinous seas incarnadine,
> Making the green one red.
>
> *Act II, Scene ii, lines 59–62*

But he is not consciously exaggerating. That is the way he feels.

Contrast his attitude with Lady Macbeth's. She says that their hands can be cleaned with a little water and that he should be ashamed to be carrying on so. She tries to make him snap out of the state he's in and get on with their plan.

Macbeth's final lines as his wife hurries him off sum up how he feels:

"To know my deed, 'twere best not know myself." [There is a knock at the gate.] / Wake Duncan with thy knocking! I would thou couldst!" (*lines 72–73*) He never thought himself capable of such evil, and he would love to be able to undo what he has done.

ACT II, SCENE III

Lines 1–20

The previous scene of horror and murder is followed by a comic scene. The Porter, one of Macbeth's servants, is awakened by the same knocking at the gate which sent Macbeth and his wife scurrying off to clean up. The Porter is still drunk from the feast. As he weaves his way to the gate, he talks to himself as if he were the porter at the gates of Hell.

The comedy of the Porter provides a contrast to the gruesome murder. By allowing the audience to relax a little, Shakespeare makes the scenes of horror even more effective.

The Porter also has a serious purpose. The little routine he makes up about being porter of "hell gate" reminds the audience of the spiritual consequences of the murder that has just been committed.

NOTE: Audiences in Shakespeare's time would recognize the "Porter of Hell-Gate" as a stock character in the so-called morality plays of the time. Morality plays were simple stories in which good was rewarded and evil was punished. So Shakespeare is, in effect, hinting that Macbeth and Lady Macbeth are not going to get away with what they have just done.

Let's take a moment to examine one of the imaginary sinners the Porter says he lets in: "here's an equivocator, that could swear in both the scales against either scale; who committed treason enough for God's sake, yet could not equivocate to heaven" (*lines 8–11*). *Equivocation* means lying, and we will soon see Macbeth and his wife doing a lot of that. But remember the Porter's speech: the liar cannot "equivocate to heaven."

Lines 21–42

Tired of his game, the Porter opens the gate. Macduff and Lennox enter, annoyed at having been kept waiting. Their scene with the Porter is classic Shakespearean "low" comedy. Low comedy is delivered by low-class characters. It is generally concerned with what we might call "bathroom humor." In this scene the Porter jokes about how liquor makes a man want to have sex but prevents him from being able to perform with a woman.

NOTE: Even in this Shakespearean "dirty joke," an important theme is being developed. The Porter's talk about liquor foreshadows what we will see about Macbeth's ambition. The more liquor a man drinks, says the Porter, the more lecherous he becomes. At the same time, he becomes less able to do anything about it. As the play progresses, the more Macbeth tries to secure his power by murder, the less secure he becomes.

Lines 42–65

Macbeth enters and learns that Macduff and Lennox have come to wake Duncan. Macbeth lies like an expert. He behaves as if it were an ordinary morning, and shows Macduff to Duncan's door. Macbeth stands aside and lets Macduff go in alone.

Lennox tells Macbeth some of the things that happened during the night. Chimneys were blown down; strange screams were heard. In fact, "Some say, the earth / Was feverous and did shake" (*lines 62–63*).

These strange events illustrate the theme of nature reflecting the state. While Macbeth committed this horrible murder, which was against the laws of human nature, and which wrecked the God-sanctioned order of things, the earth itself trembled and shook.

Macbeth's reply is humorous, though Lennox does not know it. After hearing about all the bizarre events, Macbeth says simply, " 'Twas a rough night" (*line 63*).

Lines 65–136

The murder is discovered. Macduff sounds the alarm and wakes everybody in the castle. Macbeth and Lady Macbeth do an excellent job of pretending to be innocent.

Macduff responds to the murder as an act of supernatural magnitude. Attempting to convey how horrified he is, he uses imagery from two different religions. First, Christian:

> Most sacrilegious murder hath broke ope
> The Lord's anointed temple, and stole thence
> The life o' th' building.
>
> *Act II, Scene iii, lines 9–11*

Then pagan:

> Approach the chamber, and destroy your sight
> With a new Gorgon . . .
>
> (*lines 73–74*)

There is irony in the way Macduff treats Lady Macbeth. He calls her "gentle Lady" (*line 85*) and says that his news is too harsh for a woman to hear.

Expert liar though she is, Lady Macbeth slips a bit. Her first response when she "learns" that Duncan is dead is "What, in our house!" (*line 90*). That is not really the response of a loving subject. Banquo scolds her, saying the murder would be "Too cruel anywhere" (*line 90*).

Macbeth actually seems more convincing than his wife. Could that be because he really *is* shocked and revolted by the murder he has committed? We cannot be sure, but what he says to the group is right in line with what he said in private (at the end of the last scene): "Had I but died an hour before this chance, / I had lived a blessèd time" (*lines 93–94*).

But when Duncan's sons, Malcolm and Donalbain, enter, Macbeth goes too far. He waxes poetic: "The spring, the head, the fountain of your blood / Is stopped" (*lines 100–101*) until Macduff cuts in and tells them that their father has been murdered.

NOTE: We are beginning to see that Macduff is a direct, no-nonsense sort of person. That is the most dangerous type of person to have around when, like Macbeth, you are trying to cover the truth.

Macduff seems suspicious when Macbeth says he killed Duncan's servants, who appeared to be responsible for the murder. Modern police would call that "destroying evidence." By questioning Macbeth's action, Macduff implies that things may not actually be the way they appear.

Macbeth flounders, and his wife comes to his rescue. Trying to explain why he killed the servants, Macbeth goes on at great length about how upset he was. In order to take attention off her husband, Lady Macbeth pretends to faint.

The atmosphere of suspicion is strengthened by Malcolm and Donalbain, who keep apart from the group. They stay behind when the others go to meet and decide what to do.

Lines 137–148

Malcolm and Donalbain realize that they are in danger. They decide they cannot trust anybody, and that it's wisest to run. Malcolm will go to England; Donalbain will head for Ireland.

ACT II, SCENE IV

This scene moves the action outside of Macbeth's castle for the first and only time in Act II. By doing that, Shakespeare gives us a wider perspective on the murder.

Many readers see the Old Man as a "chorus" figure. That means that, like the chorus in ancient Greek drama, he represents the common people and expresses their views.

Lines 1–19

The Old Man and Ross discuss all the strange things that have been happening since Duncan's murder. Nature itself seems upset: it is dark during the day; an owl killed a hawk (the opposite of what normally happens). Duncan's horses ate each other!

These events can be interpreted in several ways. You could say that physical nature is reacting to protest a crime that has been committed against human nature. Or, possibly, that "heaven" or "the gods" are expressing their anger. Or you can say that nature mirrors the state; that when a rightful king falls all the rest of God's order falls apart, too.

NOTE: Remember the theme of light and darkness. At this point, it seems the entire country has been plunged into darkness by Macbeth's evil deed.

Lines 20–41

Macduff enters and reports the "official version" of who committed the murder and what is going to happen. Without coming out and saying so, he makes it clear that he does not believe a word of it.

Shakespeare conveys Macduff's skepticism with great economy. Macduff, a plain-spoken man, tells his news simply. Asked who killed Duncan, he says, "Those that Macbeth hath slain." Asked why, he replies, "They were suborned" (*lines 23–24*)—they were bribed. He just gives the facts, without comment. He also reports that, because they ran away, Malcolm and Donalbain are suspected of being responsible.

Macduff doesn't bother to point out that the story sounds unlikely. Ross's responses show that he does not need any prompting to realize that it is hard to believe.

Look how Shakespeare shows that Macduff does not like what is going on: Macduff says that Macbeth has been named king and has gone to Scone to be crowned. Asked if he is going to Scone himself, Macduff replies, "No, cousin, I'll to Fife" (*line 36*)—he is going home. That is an insult to Macbeth. Without saying much, Macduff makes his attitude completely clear.

ACT III

ACT III, SCENE I

Lines 1–10

Alone, Banquo voices his suspicions about the way Macbeth gained the throne. He comes right out and says that he is afraid Macbeth "play'dst most foully for 't" (*line 3*).

Banquo is in an awkward position. He has been Macbeth's friend, but he suspects his friend of assassinating the king. For some reason, he stays at Macbeth's castle. Is that because he wants to? Or is it because Macbeth wants to keep him nearby?

Banquo also remembers that the witches who predicted a crown for Macbeth predicted that Banquo's descendents would be kings. Should that give him hope? He wonders.

Lines 11–44

Macbeth, his Queen, and their attendants enter. Macbeth invites Banquo to a feast he is holding that night.

In this scene, we see a new Macbeth. He has become very good at hiding his real feelings. As we will learn later in the scene, Macbeth is planning Banquo's murder. Yet he is gracious and friendly. Under the guise of friendship, Macbeth finds out Banquo's plans for the day. This information will help him to plan his friend's murder. Notice that Macbeth takes special interest in whether Banquo's son, Fleance, will be with Banquo when he goes riding that day.

When Banquo leaves, Macbeth says that he plans to spend the rest of the day alone until the feast. He seems every inch the monarch as he announces, "To make society / The sweeter welcome, we will keep ourself / Till supper-time alone" (*lines 41–43*).

Lines 45–72

As soon as Lady Macbeth and the others leave, Macbeth sends for men who are waiting for him outside the palace gate. When he is left alone, we learn what Macbeth is really feeling.

Macbeth is not the confident ruler he appears to be. He is tormented by fears. At the moment, those fears center on Banquo.

He has many reasons to fear his friend. Banquo has what Macbeth calls a "royalty of nature" (*line 50*). In other words, he's noble—brave, honest, and wise. That makes him dangerous to Macbeth, who depends upon his countrymen being either not smart enough to know what he's done or not brave enough to challenge him.

Besides, the fact Banquo knows about the witches threatens Macbeth. Couldn't he guess how Macbeth reacted to their prophesies? And, too, the witches predicted that Banquo's descendents would be kings. If that happened, Macbeth would have committed murder just so Banquo's children could inherit the throne. That thought drives him crazy. And maybe Macbeth wonders if Banquo is enough like him to do what *he* did to help fate along: Kill for the crown.

Lines 73–142

Macbeth arranges Banquo's murder. As we watch him manipulate the two men he has chosen to do his dirty work, we get a picture of just what a monster Macbeth has become.

First, we find out that he has already been plotting. We also see that he has been twisting the truth. He reminds the men of a previous conversation, in which he made it clear to them that Banquo is their enemy. The two men have suffered some unnamed misfortune, which was Macbeth's fault. He has told them that Banquo was really responsible. Knowing what we do about Macbeth and Banquo, we know Macbeth is lying.

NOTE: Macbeth is making skillful use of the atmosphere of paranoia that has existed since Duncan's murder. Since there's no way for the two men to know just what to believe, they might as well go along with Macbeth. He *is* the king, after all. Getting on his good side could bring them rewards.

Macbeth has also been extremely clever in choosing his murderers. They are not criminals already. They are just down on their luck. Hard times have made them desperate, so they are ready to try anything.

Macbeth arouses the two men's anger against Banquo by insulting them. Remember how Lady Macbeth prompted her husband to kill Duncan by questioning his manhood? Look at how he taunts these two:

> Ay, in the catalogue ye go for men;
> As hounds and greyhounds, mongrels, spaniels, curs,
> Sloughs, water-rugs and demi-wolves, are clept
> All by the name of dogs. . . .
>
> *Act III, Scene i, lines 92–95*

"Are you a greyhound or a mongrel?" he asks them, just as we would ask "Are you a man or a mouse?"

After insulting them, Macbeth changes tactics. He assures them that Banquo is his enemy as well as theirs. Imagine how these two men who have been enduring such hard times must feel when the king himself says, "I to your assistance do make love" (*line 124*). They are ready to do anything for him, especially kill Banquo.

Macbeth adds another condition—Fleance must be killed, too. We know, as Macbeth does, that, if Fleance survives, the witches' prediction can still come true. Having come so far, however, the two men are not held back by the idea of killing a child.

ACT III, SCENE II

This scene shows us what has happened to the relationship between Macbeth and Lady Macbeth. We remember how close they were at the beginning of the play. Macbeth rushed home to tell his wife about the witches' predictions, and everything they did, they did together.

Lines 1–7

Lady Macbeth does not know why Macbeth keeps so much to himself these days. You can tell that she is not enjoying the fruits of their murder any more than he is. But while he is concerned about Banquo, she is mainly concerned about him.

Lines 8–56

Lady Macbeth tries to get through to her husband. She scolds him for brooding so much: "Why do you keep alone, / Of sorriest fancies your companions making?" (*lines 8–9*). She sees his conscience is bothering him. As she did right after the murder, she urges him to be practical: "Things without all remedy / Should be without regard: what's done is done" (*lines 11–12*).

That may be good advice, and Macbeth probably wishes he could take it. He *is* thinking about Duncan. Macbeth says that, while he himself can't sleep because of horrible nightmares, Duncan "sleeps well" (*line* 23). Macbeth actually envies the man he killed. Since *Macbeth* is partly a morality play, it is perfectly in keeping that a good man who is dead is happier than an evil man who is still alive.

But Macbeth is not tortured only by his past. As we know, he is worried about the future, too. He reminds his wife that Banquo and Fleance are alive. Though Lady Macbeth seems more worried about whether Macbeth will be able to cover up his feelings at the banquet tonight than she is about Banquo and his son, she tries to comfort her husband. Appropriately enough for her, the comfort takes the form of reminding him that Banquo and Fleance can be killed.

Macbeth's response to that suggestion demonstrates how their relationship has changed. He hints that the murder has already been arranged, but he does not take her into his confidence. He conjures night to "Scarf up the tender eye of pitiful day" and to "tear to pieces" Banquo's fate with its "bloody and invisible hand" (*lines 47–48*).

Shakespeare suggests that Lady Macbeth is amazed by the change in her husband. Macbeth says to her, "Thou marvel'st at my words" (*line 54*). We do not know why she reacts that way, but it could very well be that she did not know he had so much evil in him.

NOTE; Trying to express how he feels, Macbeth says, "O, full of scorpions is my mind, dear wife!" (*line 36*). Can you think of any stronger way to convey his feeling? The line is made even more poignant by the fact he addresses her as "dear wife." Knowing how he feels, can you wonder why he keeps to himself?

ACT III, SCENE III

When the two men from Scene i meet to murder Banquo, a third man joins them. He says that Macbeth sent him, and the other two assume Macbeth doesn't trust them.

There is a lot of debate over just who this Third Murderer is and why he is there. In some productions, he is even played by Macbeth himself in disguise! It is more likely, though, that he is one of Macbeth's henchmen, and that he is there as an indication that Macbeth does not trust anybody.

In the attack, the First Murderer makes a mistake. When Banquo and Fleance walk into the trap that has been set for them, the Second Murderer calls for a light. The First Murderer thinks he is being told to put out the light, so he extinguishes the torch. Banquo is killed, but Fleance is able to run away in the dark.

ACT III, SCENE IV

This scene dramatizes the fact that although Macbeth and Lady Macbeth have what they wanted, they cannot enjoy it. At the royal feast they try to act the noble hosts. Reminders of their evil deeds, however, continually interrupt and ruin the evening.

Lines 1–9

The beginning of the feast gives us a chance to see Macbeth and Lady Macbeth acting the roles of king and queen. They behave formally and graciously. Macbeth instructs his guests to sit down according to their "degrees," or rank.

The two seem to enjoy their privileges. Lady Macbeth sits on her throne, staying slightly apart from the others, as befits a ruler. Macbeth mingles with "his people," but he does it as a regal gesture:

> Ourself will mingle with society
> And play the humble host.
>
> *Act III, Scene iv, lines 4–5*

Lines 10–33

The first interruption of this scene of royal graciousness occurs when the First Murderer arrives. His face has blood on it, but Macbeth is able to pull the man aside before any of the guests notice him. The murderer tells Macbeth that Banquo is dead.

You can see a big difference between Macbeth's reaction to this murder and his response to Duncan's. After killing the king, Macbeth was tortured with remorse. After having his friend killed, Macbeth is delighted.

How can a man lose his sense of right and wrong so quickly? Shakespeare seems to be suggesting that once a person gives in to the temptation of evil, his morals crumble. What ruins Macbeth's enjoyment of the news of his friend's murder is not his conscience. It is the news that Fleance was not killed too. Look at how twisted Macbeth has become; Banquo, who is dead, he calls "safe" (*line 26*), while Fleance's escape galls him. The First Murderer leaves, and Lady Macbeth reminds her husband of his duties to their guests. Macbeth tries to go back to playing the sociable host. The next interruption, however, is more serious than the first.

Macbeth must feel somewhat relieved by the news that Banquo is no longer a threat. In talking with his guests, Macbeth mentions his friend several times, saying he wishes Banquo were there. Those comments turn out to be ironic. Sitting in the seat that has been reserved for the king is Banquo's ghost, covered with gashes and blood. The ghost stares at Macbeth, who is transfixed with terror. The others cannot see the ghost, and to them Macbeth is acting like a lunatic.

NOTE: Readers disagree over whether the ghost is "real" or not. Because Macbeth is the only one who sees it, the ghost could be a figment of his imagination. Macbeth saw a dagger before his first murder, and on previous scenes he has seemed almost on the verge of a breakdown. On the other hand, if we have accepted the supernatural as real, why not this ghost? Whichever point of view you take, one thing is clear; the ghost is absolutely real to Macbeth.

The rest of the scene until the guests leave takes the form of a tug-of-war between Macbeth and Lady Macbeth. He is talking to the ghost, and she is trying to maintain appearances for their guests.

She attempts to explain away her husband's strange behavior saying he has always had these "fits." Then she takes him aside and tries to shame him into being quiet:

> Shame itself!
> Why do you make such faces? When all's done,
> You look but on a stool.
>
> *Act III, Scene iv, lines 67–69*

But Macbeth knows what he sees, and her words have little effect on him. (Remember how Macbeth could not decide whether to believe his common sense in his eyes when he saw the dagger. Now there is no contest.)

The ghost leaves, and Macbeth apologizes to his guests. His excuse—"I have a strange infirmity" (*line 87*)—has a surprising amount of truth to it. Without realizing it, he could be referring to his conscience. Though his moral sense appears to be dead, there is still some part of him that refuses to allow him to enjoy his stolen crown. But the ghost reappears, and Macbeth begins raving; he is saying way too much, and seems totally insane to his guests. He asks them how they can look at such things without being frightened. Lady Macbeth realizes she has lost control of the situation, and the evening cannot be saved. Wanting to get rid of the others before her husband says much more, she urgently tells the guests to leave. All the regal formality of the opening is now gone: "Stand not upon the order of your going / But go at once" (*lines 120–21*).

Lines 123–141

Macbeth and his wife talk after the guests leave. We learn three things: 1. Macduff refused to attend the feast, just as he refused to attend Macbeth's crowning, so Macduff is being set up as an adversary to Macbeth; 2. Macbeth is afraid, not only of Banquo but of all his lords. He says, "There's not a one of them but in his house / I keep a servant fee'd" (*lines 132–33*). In other words, he has spies. 3. Macbeth intends to visit the three witches again. Remember that the first time he met them, the evil creatures found *him*. Now he will seek *them* out. Macbeth has reached a point where he is willing to do anything; "For mine own good / All causes shall give way" (*lines 136–37*). He is no longer divided between good and evil, as he was before Duncan's murder. By killing his king, he committed himself to a path from which there is no return.

ACT III, SCENE V

The witches meet Hecate, their mistress. Many scholars believe that this scene was not actually written by Shakespeare. They see the scene as an opportunity for a song and dance from the witches.

NOTE: Whether Shakespeare wrote the scene or not, it points out an important theme: security. Hecate says, ". . . security / Is mortals' chiefest enemy" (*lines 32–33*). She means what we would call "false security." In the morality plays of Shakespeare's time, all security was seen as false security. The devil has laid many traps for mankind, they said, and if you feel secure, it is because you refuse to see the dangers. Macbeth will be given a false sense of security by the witches the next time he meets them.

ACT III, SCENE VI

We get a clear view of how the thanes of Scotland feel under Macbeth's rule in this scene. Before, we have been able to sense the atmosphere of paranoia. Here, it is demonstrated.

Lennox and another lord enter. They are having a private conversation about recent events. Notice that Lennox, who clearly means to say that something fishy is going on, has to get his message across indirectly. His speech is loaded with irony:

> The gracious Duncan
> Was pitied of Macbeth: marry, he was dead.
> And the right-valiant Banquo walked too late;
> Whom, you may say, if't please you, Fleance killed,
> For Fleance fled. Men must not walk too late.
>
> *Act III, Scene vi, lines 3–7*

Translated, he is saying, "Maybe somebody believes this, but *I* sure don't."

An important bit of news is revealed in this scene: Macduff, who is now commonly acknowledged as Macbeth's enemy, has gone to the English court. There, he intends to ask the English king for troops to help overthrow Macbeth.

Duncan's son Malcolm is already in England, where he has been treated with great respect. That gives the Scottish lords hope that the English king will be sympathetic to their plight.

After sharing the news about Macduff, Lennox and the other lord speak more directly. They yearn for relief from Macbeth's tyranny. Notice the religious imagery used by Lennox: "Some holy angel / Fly to the court of England . . . that a swift blessing / May soon return to this our suffering country / under a hand accursed!" (*lines 45–48*). That language suggests that they see Macbeth as more than just a tyrant; they consider him a devil.

ACT IV

ACT IV, SCENE I

Lines 1–38

Thunder crashes, and the witches appear. They have been out of the play since Act I, except for the unnecessary Scene V of Act III, so the beginning of this scene reminds us of who and what they are.

As the witches dance around the cauldron, they chant the recipe for the evil mess they are brewing:

> Fillet of a fenny snake,
> In the caldron boil and bake,
> Eye of newt and toe of frog,
> Wool of bat and tongue of dog
>
> *Act IV, Scene i, lines 14–17*

Their ingredients make a wonderfully nasty list, but an evil one too: "Scale of dragon . . . Witch's mummy . . . finger of birth-strangled babe. . . ." These are not just strange women; they are evil creatures.

Lines 38–43

Hecate appears. Again, Shakespeare probably did not write this section. It seems like another excuse for music and song, and it does nothing to move the plot forward.

Lines 44–135

Into this creepy, dreary fog-filled place comes Macbeth. He strides in boldly, as if he belonged there. In fact, when one of the witches senses Macbeth coming, she chants, "By the pricking of my thumbs, / Something wicked this way comes" (*lines 44–45*).

The Macbeth who presents himself to the witches is not the same man they met in Act I. That man recoiled from these weird hags, even though he was enticed by what they said. The Macbeth who comes in now is a man totally dedicated to evil.

The Macbeth the witches first waylaid was afraid of what would happen if he did something evil. (Remember how he argued with his wife in Act I, Scene vii). This Macbeth starts by announcing that even if the entire *world* falls apart as a result, he wants answers to some questions. The theme of physical nature being affected when people do sinful things that are against human nature is found in Macbeth's demand for answers:

> though the treasure
> Of nature's germens tumble all together,
> Even till destruction sicken, answer me
> To what I ask you.
>
> *Act IV, Scene i, lines 58–61*

He is saying he does not care if the order of all creation is wrecked by what he does. Remembering the weird events that followed Duncan's murder, that possibility doesn't seem so far-fetched.

Macbeth's resolve is further demonstrated when the witches give him a choice of talking with them or with their masters. Any normal person would have to think twice (at least) before asking to see the demon masters of these hags. Macbeth, however, immediately shouts, "Call 'em, let me see 'em" (*line 63*).

The witches conjure up three strange visions, and each gives Macbeth a specific piece of information:

First, an "Armed Head" appears. That means the head of a man wearing the headpiece from a suit of armor. This apparition tells Macbeth to beware Macduff, the Thane of Fife. Macbeth says that he already was worried about Macduff, but the figure vanishes.

The second apparition is a bloody child. The demon tells Macbeth to be "bloody, bold, and resolute" (*line 79*), as if Macbeth needed that advice. But he gives Macbeth a good reason to be confident: "Laugh to scorn the pow'r of man, for none of woman born / Shall harm Macbeth" (*lines 79–81*). Macbeth is pleased by this prophesy, but he plans to kill Macduff anyway.

Finally, a child wearing a crown and holding a tree in its hand appears. This figure says Macbeth will never be defeated until "Great Birnam Wood to high Dunsinane Hill / Shall come against him" (*lines 93–94*). This assurance is even more conforting to Macbeth than the previous one. You can tell that Macbeth thinks he is being told that he is invincible, but you know there has to be a trick. In this play, nothing is what it appears to be.

The form each apparition takes is an indication of doom. The Armed Head could be Macbeth's head, which Macduff will cut off. The bloody child who tells Macbeth to fear no man born of woman could be Macduff, who was "untimely ripped" from his mother's womb. (That means he was delivered in a crude version of what we today call a cesarean section. So, he was never born of a woman in the normal way.) The child with a tree in his hand might represent Malcolm, who will tell his soldiers to carry branches from the trees in Birnam Wood to disguise their approach. But Macbeth knows only what he has been told. The one warning sounds helpful, the two prophesies sound like good news to him.

There is one thing more he wants to know, though. Will Banquo's line inherit the throne? The witches do not want to answer, but Macbeth insists.

The witches show him a ghostly procession of eight kings. The last king holds a mirror, which shows even more kings. And all of them look like Banquo! Banquo himself appears, pointing at them and smiling. Macbeth interprets *this* vision correctly; the descendents of Banquo will be kings.

NOTE: This last vision serves a dramatic purpose. It enrages Macbeth and probably makes him even more evilly reckless. But there was another, nondramatic, purpose for this vision. *Macbeth* was first presented for James I, who was a descendent of the historical Banquo. "Banquo's issue," as Macbeth calls it, was the Stuart line of kings.

Lines 136–56

The witches vanish, leaving Macbeth standing amazed. Macbeth calls to Lennox, who was waiting for him nearby. Lennox says he did not see the witches go past him, confirming that they vanished into thin air. He also tells Macbeth that several men came to tell Macbeth that Macduff has gone to England.

Is Lennox toying with Macbeth in the same way the witches were? We know that Lennox was already aware of Macduff's mission to England. Perhaps he withheld the information till now for some purpose. Like the characters in the play, we cannot be sure what to believe.

Macbeth senses that it is dangerous to trust the witches: "damned [be] all those that trust them" (*line 139*). But he no longer has any cool judgment to guide him. Or maybe Macbeth considers himself damned already; he certainly places all his trust in the witches' prophesies.

In the same way that the witches' earlier predictions set the action of the first part of the play, these new prophesies have set the action of the rest.

ACT IV, SCENE II

Now that Macbeth has completed his descent from loyal thane to evil tyrant, Shakespeare leaves him for a while.

The setting changes from the eerie gloom of the witches' haunt to a quiet, domestic scene in Macduff's castle. The characters are Lady Macduff, Macduff's son, and a kinsman, the Thane of Ross.

Although Lady Macduff and her son are not part of the political turmoil caused by Macbeth, they are affected by it. Good and bad have been blurred and confused for them, too.

Lines 1–30

Macduff has gone to England without saying goodbye to his family, on whom his lack of loyalty to King

Macbeth will bring disgrace. Lady Macduff does not understand why he has abandoned them. She decides he must not love them.

NOTE: Let's stop for a minute to look at his reasons for sneaking off that way. We can guess that after enduring Macbeth's tyranny for some time, Macduff decided something had to be done. The only hope for his country was to bring back Malcolm, its rightful king. And that meant going to England in secret.

Could Macduff have guessed what would happen? It seems unlikely. He must have known that his wife and children would be shamed and unprotected, and that Macbeth would make it hard on them. But maybe he figured that a new king for Scotland was worth the price. But how could Macduff or anybody else imagine how threatened his family would be? Clearly, he underestimated Macbeth.

"How can you tell right from wrong, courage from cowardice, in a topsy-turvy world?" this scene asks. Lady Macduff is a strong, intelligent woman, and she cannot understand her husband's motives. She is angry at him, because she believes he has acted unwisely.

Ross seems convinced that Macduff is doing the right thing, but he cannot explain why. He sums up the situation well:

> But cruel are the times, when we are traitors
> And do not know ourselves; when we hold
> rumor
> From what we fear, yet know not what we fear
> *Act IV, Scene ii, lines 18–20*

Ross finds Macduff's family's plight so sad, he has to leave before he starts crying.

Lines 31–64

Lady Macduff tells her son that his father is dead. What she means is that they have been left to fend for themselves; nobody knows when Macduff will come back.

The tone of the scene is light, but the intent is serious. Macduff's son is bright and cocky. He doesn't believe for a minute that his father is dead. Probably Lady Macduff's tone lets him know that she does not mean what she says literally. But being left alone and in disgrace will be difficult for them.

Lady Macduff also tells her son that his father is a traitor. She probably says it because she knows that he will hear a lot of other people say it before long.

Lines 65–85

Not even the oppressed people of Scotland realize the depth of Macbeth's evil. Never in Lady Macduff's talks with Ross or with her son has it occurred to any of them that she and her children could be killed. That would be too cruel, even for Macbeth.

This false sense of security is shattered when a man runs in, winded and scared to death. He warns Lady Macduff that she and her family are in great danger. Then he runs away. Lady Macduff has only a few moments to wonder why she should be in danger when she has done no harm before several murderers enter.

One of the murderers says the same thing about Macduff his wife has just been saying—that he is a traitor. This time, both she and her son defend him. When the young Macduff is grabbed by the man and stabbed, he bravely calls to his mother to run. She does, but she is caught by another murderer and killed.

ACT IV, SCENE III

In England, Malcolm and Macduff repair the bonds of loyalty and trust which have been destroyed by Macbeth.

Lines 1–37

Macduff wants Malcolm to lead a revolt against Macbeth. Malcolm would like to overthrow his father's murderer, but he has a problem: how does he know he can trust Macduff?

Malcolm is in a delicate position. As Scotland's rightful king, he owes it to his people to overthrow the tyrant. But he must be very careful. Macbeth has been sending spies to try to lure Malcolm back to Scotland and into a trap. So far, Malcolm has seen through all their plots.

Now Malcolm has to figure out whether or not Macduff is what he appears to be. In Macduff's favor is the fact that he is known as an honest man. But Macbeth was considered an honest man at one time. Also, Macbeth has not actually done Macduff any personal harm yet. (Neither of them knows about the murder of Macduff's family.)

Malcolm's problem is how to tell a good man from a bad man acting good: "Though all things foul would wear the brows of grace, / Yet grace must still look so" (*lines 24–25*). In other words, "foul" wants to *seem* "fair," and "fair" is "fair" by nature, so how can you tell them apart?

Fortunately for Malcolm, he has a quick mind and a clever tongue. When one approach fails, he can try another. His direct questioning of Macduff ("Wouldn't you get a lot for turning me in to Macbeth?" "If you are Macbeth's enemy, how can you have left your family exposed to him?") only makes the older man angry. That does not help. Macduff's anger could be either that of a guilty man found out or an innocent man unjustly accused.

Lines 137–139

Malcolm tries another tactic. He tells lies about himself. He describes in great detail what an awful person he is and what a terrible king he would make.

At first, Macduff tries to downplay the faults Malcolm gives himself. After all, Macduff thinks, anybody would be better than Macbeth.

As Malcolm goes on, he gives an anatomy of a bad king. He says that he is lustful. Macduff does not approve, but he knows that there are plenty of women willing to satisfy a king's sexual appetites.

Malcolm adds greed to his list of faults. Macduff likes this fault even less, but says that there are enough riches in Scotland to satisfy anybody's desire for wealth. Malcolm's virtues, says Macduff, will outweigh his faults.

Malcolm gives Macduff one final chance to reject him. He lists every virtue a king could have. Then he declares that he doesn't have *any* of them. He says that, if he were king, he would "Pour the sweet milk of concord into hell" (*line 98*).

That is just what Macbeth has done. Finally, Macduff sees that Malcolm would not be an improvement. He gives up hope.

By giving up hope, Macduff passes Malcolm's test. Malcolm reveals that he has been telling lies about himself in order to test Macduff. The truth, he says, is just the opposite. Because of the extremity of the situation, we can forgive Malcolm for his lack of humility as he informs Macduff of his virtues.

"Old Siward, with ten thousand warlike men" (*line 134*) are already prepared to march on Scotland, Malcolm tells Macduff.

Lines 139–159

This interlude about the king of England and his healing powers serves to contrast with the sickness a bad king like Macbeth brings on his country. The imagery is religious: "How he solicits heaven, Himself best knows" (*lines 149–150*), suggesting that a true king is good, and a gift from God.

Lines 160–192

Ross appears, having just arrived from Scotland. He is bringing the terrible news about Macduff's family, but he cannot bring himself to say it at first.

NOTE: Notice that when Ross first enters, Malcolm does not recognize him. Macbeth has kept the rightful king away from his country for so long that he does not even know his people anymore. Of course, after riding hard for several days to be the bearer of bad news, Ross may not look his best!

When Ross describes Scotland, it sounds as if he were trying to tell somebody about a nightmare:

> Where sighs, and groans, and shrieks that rent the air,
> Are made, not marked; where violent sorrow seems
> A modern ecstasy.
>
> *Act IV, Scene iii, lines 168–170*

Ross is going through his own personal nightmare trying to bring himself to tell Macduff that his wife and children have been killed. When Macduff asks about his family, Ross dodges the question. His answer has a weird blend of horror and humor:

> *Macduff:* The tyrant has not battered at their peace?
> *Ross:* No; they were well at peace when I did leave 'em.
>
> *Act IV, Scene iii, lines 178–79*

Macduff can tell that Ross is holding something back. He presses him for news.

Ross changes the subject for a moment, saying that he has seen Macbeth's army. He appeals to Malcolm to come home and lead the revolt. When he is told that the troops are ready to march, he knows that he can no longer wait to tell Macduff about his family.

Lines 192–240

Macduff's reaction to the news is the most touching passage in the play for many readers. This blunt, practical man, this soldier who has seen many of his comrades die on the field, stands blinking in disbelief. He must ask Ross to tell him several times. He can understand the words but he cannot fathom anything so horrible.

There is a lesson in the way Macduff takes the news. Malcolm, who is still relatively inexperienced, tries to snap Macduff out of his grief:

> *Malcolm:* Dispute it like a man.
> *Macduff:* I shall do so;
> But I must also feel it as a man.
> *Act IV, Scene iii, lines 220–21*

Macduff is not only brave in fighting. He is brave enough to face his own personal tragedy.

Finally, Macduff converts his grief to rage. Strong as his resolve to overthrow Macbeth was before, it is now even stronger.

NOTE: Shakespeare has just set up the last act of the play. We know that Macbeth is depending on the witches' new prophesies and believes himself invincible. We also know that a mighty army is setting out from England to defeat him. The stage is set for the final battle, in Act V.

ACT V

ACT V, SCENE I

The scene shifts back to Scotland and Macbeth's castle. Lady Macbeth makes her last appearance in the play.

In this scene, Lady Macbeth is entirely lost in a nightmare world. This is one of the most famous scenes in all Shakespeare. It is usually called "the sleepwalking scene."

Lines 1–20

Lady Macbeth's Gentlewoman—her maid—and the Doctor prepare us for what is coming. The Gentlewoman has seen Lady Macbeth walk in her sleep every night since Macbeth left the castle with his army. Tonight, she has asked the Doctor to watch the strange ritual with her. The Gentlewoman says that she would not dare repeat what she has heard Lady Macbeth say while sleepwalking.

Lines 21–72

Lady Macbeth enters, carrying a candle. Her eyes are open, but, as the Gentlewoman says, "their sense are shut" (*line 28*).

In her nightmare, Lady Macbeth relives the murders she and her husband have committed. She talks to her husband, repeating assurances she has given him: "What need we fear who knows it, when none can call our power to accompt?" (*lines 40–42*), and "I tell you yet again, Banquo's buried" (*lines 66–67*).

These words take on a horrible irony in this context. Obviously, she is tortured by fear. Have terror and guilt worried away an evil character? Or was the confidence she showed earlier in the play just an act for her husband's sake? Perhaps she even fooled herself, and these nightmares are her subconscious mind making her face the truth.

NOTE: Shakespeare, of course, would not have known about modern psychological concepts like "subconscious mind." Yet it appears that he instinctively understood what psychologists tell us: that emotions we suppress come back to harm us.

What is even more ironic, as she sleepwalks Lady Macbeth compulsively makes motions as if she were washing her hands. She says, "who would have thought the old man to have had so much blood in him?" (*lines 42–43*), and "Here's the smell of the blood still" (*line 53*). Remember how she had assured Macbeth that they could easily wash their hands and be "clear[ed] of the deed"?

Lines 73–84

After Lady Macbeth returns to bed, the Doctor and the Gentlewoman talk about what they have seen.

The Doctor says something that sums up one of the major themes of the play: that of evil as a perversion of nature. "Unnatural deeds / Do breed unnatural troubles" (*lines 75–76*). Macbeth and Lady Macbeth got what they wanted by committing deeds that went against God's laws and human nature. For a time, they seemed to get away with it. Now they are paying the price.

ACT V, SCENE II

Shakespeare begins the build up to the final battle. Like modern movies do, he will "cut" from scene to scene—back and forth between scenes showing the English forces that are approaching Macbeth's castle and scenes showing Macbeth preparing for their attack.

This short scene among the Scottish thanes gets across several plot points: 1. the English army is near, led by Malcolm, Macduff, and Siward; 2. the invaders will meet the Scottish forces near Birnam Wood (remember the prophesy); 3. Malcolm's brother, Donalbain, is not with them. (You can consider him a loose thread in the plot: he never reappears.)

The second half of the scene touches on several important points.

Menteith picks up the theme of "unnatural deeds" when he says of Macbeth "all that is within him does condemn / Itself for being there" (*lines 24–25*). That statement is based on the idea that human nature is fundamentally good. Therefore, the evil deeds Macbeth has committed have made him fight with his own nature.

Now that the trust that Macbeth destroyed for a time has been repaired by Macduff and Malcolm, a theme of loyalty begins to emerge. Malcolm and Macduff lead an army that is fueled by a strong cause: to revenge the wrongs committed by Macbeth. Macbeth's army, on the other hand, moves "only in command, / Nothing in love" (*lines 19–20*).

ACT V, SCENE III

Seeing Macbeth back at his castle, we can understand why even those followers who have stuck with him do not love him, as subjects should love a king. He raves like a madman, talking about how invincible and unafraid he is. His boasts sound empty: "the heart I bear / Shall never sag with doubt nor shake with fear" (*lines 9–10*).

Macbeth has not lost touch with reality completely, though. In a quieter moment, he reflects on all he has given up. He seems to sense that his life is nearly over. What he says to the Doctor (or to himself, depending on how you read it) is touching:

> And that which should accompany old age,
> As honor, love, obedience, troops of friends,
> I must not look to have; but, in their stead,
> Curses not loud but deep . . .
>
> *Act V, Scene iii, lines 24–27*

Do you feel sorry for him, or do you see him as a monster who is getting what he deserves?

Seyton actually seems to be making fun of Macbeth when he enters and asks, "What's your gracious pleasure?" (*line 29*). Seyton confirms a report that ten thousand soldiers are approaching.

Macbeth is terrified but determined not to admit it. He commands Seyton to help him put on his armor, even though it is not really needed yet, but ten lines later he is snapping at Seyton to help him take it off.

Macbeth sounds very different when he asks the doctor about his wife. She is sick, with "thick-coming fantasies." Macbeth asks the Doctor if he can cure her: "Canst thou not minister to a mind diseased?" (*line 40*). But he knows the Doctor's answer before he hears it. She is beyond all help.

Macbeth demonstrates that even he doesn't realize the extent of his evil and the destruction it has caused. He wishes the Doctor could cure Scotland of its disease. He is talking about the invading army from England.

NOTE: Actually, Macbeth *himself* is the cause of Scotland's disease. The image of Macbeth as a bringer of disease is made even sharper by our memory of the

English king's ability to heal disease. Appropriately, the English troops are coming to heal Scotland's disease by overthrowing Macbeth.

ACT V, SCENE IV

The scene shifts to Malcolm, Macduff, and the English troops, now united with the Scottish thanes. In a short scene, one important plot point and several thematic points are brought out.

Malcolm gives an order that makes one of the witches' prophesies come true. He orders each soldier to cut a branch from a tree in Birnam Wood and carry it in front of him, to disguise their movements.

Something Malcolm says to his troops points up the theme of loyalty. Referring to Macbeth, he says, "none serve with him but constrainèd things / Whose hearts are absent too" (*lines 13–14*).

Malcolm also promises that confusion will soon come to an end:

> The time approaches,
> That will with due decision make us know
> What we shall say we have and what we owe.
>
> *Act V, Scene iv, lines 16–18*

In other words, the battle will decide whether Malcolm's claim to the throne is still all words or whether he will really be king.

ACT V, SCENE V

Lines 1–28

Macbeth, in Dunsinane, is puffing himself up with thoughts about how impregnable the castle is. If so many Scottish soldiers had not gone over to Malcolm, he says, he could have met the invaders openly. As it is, he plans to stay put—and let them try to come and get him.

Then offstage, some women scream. Alone while Seyton goes to investigate, Macbeth reflects grimly how unstartled he was at that sound: he has trained himself to horrors so completely. Seyton returns and announces, "The Queen, my lord, is dead." Macbeth's first words are "She should have died hereafter/ There would have been a time for such a word."

What is he saying? Readers disagree. You can argue that Macbeth means, "She should have waited to die. I'm busy now"; that he has lost feeling now even for her. Or you can read the lines as "She would have died inevitably, as we all do. But there would have been time for grief another day." Whether inspired by grief or by total indifference, what follows is an eloquent rush of despair. Day after day after interminable day, our lives creep along to our dusty deaths, he says. And then: "Out, out, brief candle!"—enough of life! He calls life a pathetic, strutting actor briefly on a stage, and then says:

> It is a tale
> Told by an idiot, full of sound and fury
> Signifying nothing.
>
> *Act V, Scene v, lines 26–28*

Lines 29–52

A messenger enters with news Macbeth never imagined he would hear: it looks as if the wood is on the move.

Macbeth rages at the man, but sees he is lost. He calls his troops out, and says, bitterly, "I 'gin to be a weary of the sun" (*line 49*)—he is ready to die.

He is a savage, doomed man, but you can see the wreckage of nobility in him. It is chilling to hear his battle cry:

> Blow wind, come wrack!
> At least we'll die with harness on our back.
>
> *Act V, Scene v, lines 51–52*

ACT V, SCENE VI

Malcolm's forces arrive outside Macbeth's castle carrying branches from Birnam Wood. The final battle is now only moments away.

Malcolm's order to his troops has a symbolic significance: "Your leavy screens throw down, / And show like those you are." Under Malcolm's reign, things will be what they appear to be. The confusion caused by Macbeth's evil will be banished from the land.

ACT V, SCENE VII

The English forces attack, and the battle begins. Somewhere on the field, Macbeth encounters Old Siward's son. They fight and young Siward is killed.

Young Siward is courageous. Macbeth expects the young soldier to run when he finds out who he is facing. Instead, he bravely attacks Macbeth.

Macbeth seems almost unwilling to fight, but he has no choice. We can almost pity him. He is trapped and despairing. Life has no meaning for him, but pride makes him fight on.

Macbeth leaves, and Macduff passes through. He has only one thought: to find and kill Macbeth.

Next, Malcolm and Old Siward appear. The battle is almost won, they say. What few followers Macbeth has left are fighting halfheartedly.

ACT V, SCENE VIII

Lines 1–34

Malcolm and Old Siward leave, and Macbeth reappears. He knows he has lost, and he remembers the Roman custom of the defeated commander dying on his own sword. But Macbeth refuses to do that. He will fight to the end.

The end arrives in the person of Macduff. He addresses Macbeth as a devil, saying, "Turn, hell-hound, turn!"

Oddly enough, Macbeth seems to soften. Is he afraid? He *was* warned to "beware Macduff." Or does some remaining shred of humanity in his nature hold him back? "My soul is too much charged / With blood of thine already," he tells Macduff. Macbeth's words and behavior suggest that he actually regrets the murder of Macduff's family, but he cannot undo what has been done.

Macbeth must expect Macduff to be frightened when he warns him that he lives a "charmèd" life, which must not yield / To one of woman born." Instead, Macduff laughs at him. Macduff was not born of woman in the normal way; he was pulled from his mother's womb before he was due.

Now there can be no doubt in Macbeth's mind that the end has arrived. He knows that by trusting the hags who seemed to be offering him his heart's desire, he has thrown away his honor, his dignity, his life, and his soul.

For a moment, Macbeth seems to want to save his life; he seems scared. He refuses to fight. In response, Macduff says:

> We'll have thee, as our rarer monsters are,
> Painted upon a pole, and underwrit,
> "Here may you see the tyrant."
>
> *Act V, Scene viii, lines 25–27*

That humiliation Macbeth is too proud to bear, and he chooses to fight for whatever last shred of dignity he can salvage. Reaching deep inside himself, he finds some of the courage for which he was so admired at the beginning of the play:

> Lay on, Macduff;
> And damned be him that first cries "Hold, enough!"
>
> *Act V, Scene viii, lines 33–34*

He and Macduff fight, and Macbeth is killed.

Lines 35–53

With Macbeth dead, the remainder of the play is devoted to establishing new order. Themes of honor and loyalty dominate this section.

Malcolm, Old Siward, the thanes, and the soldiers enter and survey the battleground. The dead and wounded are still being counted. Clearly, however, the day has been a great success for their side.

Old Siward is told that his son has been killed in battle. Shakespeare uses Siward's reaction to his son's death to point up the theme of honor. Siward wants to know if Young Siward was wounded in the front of his body. (That is where he would be wounded if he was fighting. If he were running away, he would have been wounded in the back.) Told that his son's wounds are in the front, he says he is not grieved. He is proud, because his son died a good soldier's death.

Some of us who read the play today might question Old Siward's readiness to accept his son's death. But one thing is clear: he has a code of honor, and he lives by it.

Malcolm's attitude suggests that he will be a good king. He insists that Young Siward is "worth more sorrow."

Lines 53–75

Macduff enters, carrying Macbeth's head. He hails Malcolm as king of Scotland. Macbeth's death brings only joy to his people.

NOTE: You might wonder at some point what has happened to Fleance and all of Banquo's royal sons that Macbeth saw in the witches' caldron. It is never spelled out in the play, but we're meant to believe that the crown will fall into Banquo's family line sometime later—in another generation. And, needless to say, it will follow naturally and honorably.

Malcolm's speech ends the play on an optimistic note. The rightful king will now assume the throne, and he will be a good and loving ruler.

The first thing Malcolm does is acknowledge how much he owes to the thanes. Remember that his father, who was a good king, went out of his way to show love and gratitude to those who served him well.

To reward the thanes, Malcolm starts by making them earls. That action is significant. Under Macbeth, Scotland became barbaric. Malcolm is saying that under his rule, the land will become more civilized.

We learn from Malcolm that Lady Macbeth is thought to have committed suicide. She has come to the most ignoble end possible.

With Malcolm's crowning the right and natural order of things is restored. Malcolm has God's blessing. He says he will do all that is required of him "by the grace of Grace" and "in measure, time, and place."

The play concludes with Malcolm's invitation to his people to see him crowned at Scone. We can bet that, unlike when Macbeth went to Scone for the same purpose, Macduff will be there to pay honor to his rightful king.

A STEP BEYOND

Tests and Answers

TESTS

Test 1

1. Macbeth won the respect of King Duncan by _____
   A. slaying the traitor Macdonwald
   B. serving as a gracious host for his king
   C. not pleading for advancement

2. King Duncan rewarded Macbeth by dubbing him _____
   A. the Earl of Sinel
   B. the Thane of Cawdor
   C. Bellona's bridegroom

3. In addressing Banquo, the witches called him _____
   I. lesser than Macbeth, and greater
   II. not so happy as Macbeth, yet much happier
   III. a future father of kings
   A. I and II B. I and III
   C. I, II, and III

4. When Macbeth said, "Two truths are told / As happy prologues" he was referring to _____
   A. his titles of Glamis and Cawdor
   B. the victories against the kerns and gallowglasses
   C. the predictions made to Banquo and to himself

5. "Nothing in his life / Became him like the leaving it" is a reference to _____
   A. the traitorous Thane of Cawdor
   B. Banquo's son, Fleance
   C. Duncan's son, Donalbain

6. Duncan's statement, "I have begun to plant thee and will labour / To make thee full of growing" is an example of _____
   A. a simile B. a metaphor
   C. personification

7. Lady Macbeth characterizes her husband as being _____
   A. "the glass of fashion and the mould of form"
   B. "too full of the milk of human kindness"
   C. "a cannon overcharg'd with a double crack"

8. Macbeth agonizes over the possible killing of the king by saying _____
   I. he is my house guest; I should protect him
   II. Duncan's virtues will "plead like angels"
   III. "I am his kinsman and his subject"
   A. I and III B. II and III
   C. I, II, and III

9. Macbeth's statement to his wife, "Bring forth men-children only" signifies that he _____
   A. is proud of his wife's transformation
   B. is concerned over the succession to the throne
   C. has accepted the challenge to slay the king

10. As part of the plan to kill the king, Lady Macbeth would _____
    A. get the chamberlains drunk
    B. smear Duncan's face with blood
    C. arrange an alibi for Macbeth

11. Trace Macbeth's transformation from a good man to an evil man.

12. What motivates Macbeth to take the evil path he chooses?

13. What influence do the witches have on Macbeth?

14. Contrast Macbeth's response to the witches' predictions with Banquo's.

15. Describe the relationship between Macbeth and Lady Macbeth. Trace how it changes over the course of the play.

Test 2

1. "Art thou not, fatal vision, sensible / To feeling as to sight?" is a reference to the _____
   A. ghost of Banquo B. dagger
   C. bubbling cauldron

2. Lady Macbeth confessed that she would have killed King Duncan herself except for the fact that _____
   A. she couldn't gain easy access to his bedchamber
   B. he looked like her father
   C. one of Duncan's guards spied her on the stairway

3. Shakespeare introduced the Porter in order to _____
   A. allow Macduff to gain admission to the castle

B. remind the audience of the Witches' prophecies
C. provide comic relief

4. Malcolm and Donalbain flee after the murder ____
A. because they fear the daggers in men's smiles
B. in order to join Macduff in England
C. lest they be blamed for it

5. Macbeth arranges for Banquo's death by telling the hired killers that ____
A. Banquo had thwarted their careers
B. if they fail, they will pay with their own lives
C. he will eradicate all records of their previous crimes

6. Macbeth startles his dinner guests by ____
A. conversing with the Ghost of Banquo
B. attempting to wash the blood from his hands
C. saying to Lady Macbeth that, "Murder will out."

7. The Witches threw into the cauldron ____
I. eye of newt and toe of frog
II. wool of bat and tongue of dog
III. fang of snake and eagle's glare
A. I and II B. I and III C. II and III

8. The three apparitions which appeared to Macbeth were ____
I. an armed head
II. a child with a crown
III. a bloody child
A. I and II B. II and III
C. I, II, and III

9. In Act IV, Malcolm is at first lukewarm toward Macduff because he _____
   A. wasn't prepared to overthrow Macbeth
   B. suspects a trick
   C. wasn't worthy of becoming king, in his opinion

10. Birnam Wood comes to Dunsinane when _____
   A. the witches rendezvous with Macbeth
   B. the camouflaged soldiers make their advance
   C. Lady Macbeth convinces her husband to stand and fight

11. What is the significance of the line "Fair is foul, and foul is fair" (*I, i, 10*)?

12. How does *Macbeth* function as a morality play?

13. How does Shakespeare use the technique of dramatic irony in *Macbeth?*

14. How does Lady Macbeth overcome her husband's resistance to the idea of killing King Duncan?

15. Contrast Macduff's response to the news of his wife's and children's deaths with Macbeth's response to being told Lady Macbeth is dead.

ANSWERS

Test 1

1. A **2.** B **3.** C **4.** A **5.** A **6.** B

7. B **8.** C **9.** C **10.** A

11. First, give evidence to prove that Macbeth *is* a good man at the beginning of the play. The strongest evidence is to be found in the way other people think of him. In Act I, Scene ii his courage is highly praised. The bloody soldier obviously admires his captain, and Duncan is moved when he is told of Macbeth's exploits. Quote the references to "brave Macbeth" and "noble Macbeth."

Look at Macbeth's relationship with Banquo. Banquo is as honest and open a man as you will find. Give examples from Act I, Scene iii, that suggest that Banquo considers Macbeth a trusted friend.

Now you have established that he is well thought of by his peers. Does this prove that he is actually a good man? Not entirely. How can we examine what is in his heart? Quote what Lady Macbeth says about him in Act I, Scene v. She says his nature is "too full o' th' milk of human kindness." She does not mean it as a compliment; she is evaluating the obstacles in her path. So she is probably telling the truth.

Macbeth's reaction to the prophesy that he will be king is an important clue. He calls it a "suggestion / Whose horrid image doth unfix my hair" (*lines 134–135*). A wicked man would be delighted at the idea. Macbeth is horrified. Therefore, you have established that Macbeth has a conscience.

Now show how his conscience works on him up through Duncan's murder, trying to hold him back from killing the king. Act I, Scene vii (both his soliloquy and his scene with Lady Macbeth), and Act II, Scenes i and ii, will supply all the information you need.

After Duncan is dead, Macbeth changes. He suffers, but now he seems to suffer not from fear of doing wrong but from fear of losing what he has gained through wrongdoing. Contrast Macbeth's attitude towards Duncan's murder with his attitude toward Banquo's.

Macbeth demonstrates that he has lost all sense of good and evil after the banquet scene. Quote Act III, Scene iv, lines 136–137: "For mine own good / All causes shall give way." His actions after that statement prove that he really has no "milk of human kindness" left. Give examples, such as the cold-blooded murder of Macduff's wife and children and, depending on how you read it, his reaction to Lady Macbeth's death.

12. Macbeth is motivated by his ambition to be king. Show how that motivation is first revealed and how it operates throughout the play. Examine how Macbeth responds to the witches' prophecy that he will be king. Quote Banquo's references to Macbeth's being "rapt." Contrast Macbeth's reaction with Banquo's, demonstrating that Macbeth has a powerful desire to possess the crown.

It seems as if Macbeth never would go through with the murder if Lady Macbeth did not insist on it. In his soliloquy in Act I, Scene vii, however, Macbeth does not hide behind that excuse. He says, "I have no spur / To prick the sides of my intent, but only / Vaulting ambition" (*lines 25–27*). From the rest of the play, show how keeping the crown has become more important to him than anything else in life.

13. The point here is to investigate both the nature of the witches' power over Macbeth and the limits of that power. The section on the witches in the "Characters" section of this guide will help you.

First, establish that they have the supernatural ability to foretell the future. Quote their prophesies, and show how no mortal could have known those things. You can do this for the predictions both in Act I and Act IV.

Next, show what Macbeth does as a consequence. It is not hard to demonstrate that they have not made him do anything. He has just taken a suggestion that he finds appealing.

You can also point out how they deceive him. This is clearest in the second set of prophesies. List each prediction and tell how Macbeth interprets it as help or comfort. Then show what actually happens. The section of the scene-by-scene analysis devoted to Act IV, Scene i, will help you.

14. What you are really contrasting is how two different people respond to temptation. There are two parts to their responses: how they respond immediately, and what they do as a consequence.

Macbeth's first response is fear; we learn that from Banquo. Then use quotes from his soliloquy in Act I, Scene iii, to demonstrate how deeply the idea of becoming king has touched him.

Banquo's immediate response is skeptical. Quote the way he teases the witches in Act I, Scene iii, and the cautious advice he gives Macbeth a few lines later. Macbeth's later actions reveal that he's taken to heart what he has been told. He begins plotting to murder the king, and when Banquo brings up the witches he lies and says he does not think about them.

Use Act II, Scene i, to clarify what Banquo thinks about witches' predictions. He has not just put them out of his mind. After all, one prophesy has come true. But he can refer to them openly, and tells Macbeth that he dreamed about the "weird sisters."

In his soliloquy in Act III, Scene i, Banquo reveals that he would like it if the witches were right and his descendents would be kings. Never at any time, however, does he consider compromising his integrity to make that happen.

15. At the beginning, they treat each other as equals. They have great concern for each other. He races to tell her the news about the witches; she immediately begins plotting how to gain her husband his heart's desire. Show how the murder of Duncan is a product of teamwork.

They have a very close relationship. Macbeth addresses his wife affectionately as "my dearest partner in greatness" and "dearest love." She demonstrates how well she knows her husband—his desires and his nature. Show how her speech in Act I, Scene vii, is an accurate evaluation of Macbeth's ambition and of the way his nature will hold him back.

Lady Macbeth seems the more resolute of the two. What is interesting is that her taunting enables her husband to get something he really wants very badly.

Once Duncan is dead and Macbeth is irrevocably committed to a course of evil, Lady Macbeth fades into the background. Give several instances in which he goes off on his own course without consulting her. Show how, cut off from him, she descends into madness.

Test 2

1. B **2.** B **3.** C **4.** A **5.** A **6.** A

7. A **8.** C **9.** B **10.** B

11. This line in the first scene tips us off that things will not be what they appear to be. Often, they will be just the opposite. This is a major motif in the play, and examples are numerous. Cite several.

Point out that Macbeth's first line echoes almost exactly the witches' chant: "So foul and fair a day I have not seen." When the witches appear and tell Macbeth he will be king, Banquo asks why he seems afraid of things that "sound so fair?" We will learn that the "fair" news is actually foul. Macbeth *will* become king, and in doing so he will commit himself to a path of evil which will mean his death, and ironically, Banquo's.

Choose several other examples and treat them the same way. You may want to focus on Lady Macbeth's instructions to her husband in Act I, Scene v, to "look like th' innocent flower, / But be the serpent under't" (*lines 66–67*). In other words, "look fair to cover your foul intentions." Show how she does exactly that when she greets Duncan and his party in the next scene.

Other examples you can use are pointed out in the "Themes" section and the scene-by-scene analysis.

You can also show how Macbeth's sense of good and evil is so corrupted that by the end "foul" and "fair" are indistinguishable to him.

12. Morality plays taught simple moral lessons. They depicted the struggle between the forces of good and evil to possess men's souls.

The story of *Macbeth* is a warning to anybody who considers trying to get what he wants by doing something he knows is wrong. It cautions us that the most appealing temptations are often the most horrible traps. To show how the play gets that message across, chart how Macbeth is destroyed by giving in to temptation.

Macbeth is hoodwinked by the witches, As you did in Question 3 of Test 1, list the things they tell him. Describe how each prediction is like a delicious-looking apple which is actually poisoned.

Read the scene-by-scene analysis for Act III, Scene v, for a discussion of how the witches give Macbeth a false sense of security. Security was a major theme of morality plays.

The play also makes it clear that Macbeth is destroyed because evil is like a disease. Once you let it into your system, it will eat away at your insides until it kills you. Show how each murder necessitates another, and how none of the killings makes Macbeth feel any better.

13. Remember that dramatic irony is present when the audience knows something the characters, or some of the characters, do not.

When Duncan and his party arrive at Macbeth's castle, they are unaware of the wicked plans that are being made. Their lighthearted, joking mood is ironic to us, because we know what they are really walking into. The scene-by-scene analysis for Act I, Scene vi, details the use of dramatic irony in this scene.

Dramatic irony enriches the last act of the play. Macbeth has become a monster, but he's also become a pathetic figure. His desperation is obvious. Ten thousand troops are on their way to overthrow him; his own troops are deserting. And he places his confidence in the weird sisters—the hags whose suggestion that he would be king got him into this mess! We can see that he is doomed, but he cannot. He fights on, talking about his "charmed life." His failure (or refusal) to see what is obvious to us makes the end of the play much more powerful than it would be otherwise.

Give several other examples of dramatic irony. You might use the scene after Duncan's murder, beginning with Macduff's entrance and continuing through the discovery of the crime. Find other examples.

14. Lady Macbeth's resolution stands out in sharp contrast to Macbeth's wavering. One way she overcomes him is through sheer determination. Find several quotes from Act I, Scene vii, in which she makes him feel the strength of her determination. (Look at lines 54–59, for example.)

She is not above insulting her husband to rouse him to action. Since she is his wife, her comments which question his manhood have an added kick.

Finally, she neutralizes his fears with her practicality. After the murder she says, " 'Tis the eye of childhood / That fears a painted devil" (*Act II, Scene ii, lines 54–55*). Find other ways in which she attempts to quiet his over-active imagination, or his visions.

15. The essential contrast is between a good, righteous man and a morally bankrupt one. Each man's response can be divided into three parts: 1. hearing the news; 2. accepting the news, and 3. what he does after.

Examine the three stages for both men. Contrast how Macduff, who is virtuous, cannot believe the news at first. Once he accepts it, he feels the pain sharply. Macbeth, on the other hand, seems unsurprised and it is hard to tell if he feels any pain; life is meaningless, he says quickly, and everybody dies. Show the direction Macduff takes (a quest for righteous revenge). Compare it with the final, desperate, suicidal stand taken by Macbeth.

Conclude by pointing out what we learn about the soul-destroying nature of evil by contrasting the two responses.

Term Paper Ideas

The Nature of Evil

1. How does the play portray evil as a perversion of human nature? Show how Macbeth and Lady Macbeth have to go against their own natures in order to kill Duncan. Trace the effect the betrayal of human nature has on each of them.

2. How does the imagery of disease function in *Macbeth?* Trace the way in which evil works on Macbeth and on Scotland like a sickness. Find imagery to support the idea that Malcolm and Macduff "heal" the country by overthrowing Macbeth.

3. What makes Macbeth susceptible to evil? Explore the nature of Macbeth's ambition, and show how it overrides his sense of right and wrong.

4. Evil within vs. evil without. Is evil an outside force, or does it come from within a person? Find instances in the play to support either theory, or both.

5. How is Macbeth destroyed by evil? Trace the path of Macbeth's downfall and show how it happens as a consequence of his murdering Duncan.

6. As Macbeth becomes more evil, how do his feelings change? Start by exploring how his feelings at the beginning of the play are much like anybody else's. Trace the way in which his feelings about people and his responses to events become twisted and abnormal.

7. Trace how Lady Macbeth is destroyed by evil. Show how she renounces all human feeling in Act I and seems to be successful. After the murder, follow her downward course into madness and death.

8. How does evil work by deception? Contrast what Macbeth and Lady Macbeth believe they are gaining through murder with what they actually get. Do they deceive themselves, or are they deceived by others?

9. How can evil be avoided? Macbeth gives in to temptation. Take several characters who maintain their integrity and investigate what the play says about how they do it.

10. How does Shakespeare establish the atmosphere of evil which pervades *Macbeth*? Start with the witches, and show how their presence reflects on all the events of the play. Give examples of how the imagery in the language creates a feeling of evil. Also examine the setting.

The Supernatural

1. How does Macbeth's changing attitude toward the supernatural reflect the change in his character? Contrast Macbeth's reaction to the witches when he first sees them with his attitude toward them in Act IV.

2. Supernatural events occur throughout the play. Discuss their dramatic function. Each time Macbeth encounters something supernatural—the witches, the floating dagger, a ghost—he moves more deeply into evil. List the supernatural events and comment on how each marks a step in Macbeth's downfall.

3. Do the supernatural events really occur, or are they projections of Macbeth's inner state? Some readers believe that the floating dagger, Banquo's ghost, and even the witches are products of Macbeth's imagination. Explore that possibility. Point out in what way, if any, the meaning of the play is changed by accepting or rejecting the reality of the supernatural.

4. How do the witches' predictions influence Macbeth's actions? Analyze what they tell Macbeth at the beginning of the play. How do they win his confidence? Why do those particular prophesies have such an effect on him? Do the same for the second set of predictions.

5. Nature itself reacts to some of the events in a supernatural manner. Explore how the theme of good vs. evil is supported by such occurrences. "Good" in the play is not relative; it is absolute. Give examples in which nature itself seems to be condemning an evil action.

The Characters

1. Describe the way Macbeth and Lady Macbeth influence each other in the play. What effect does Lady Macbeth's determination to kill Duncan have on her husband? After the murder, how does Macbeth change, and how does that affect Lady Macbeth?

2. Contrast Macbeth's imaginative nature with Lady Macbeth's pragmatic nature. Compare their attitudes toward Duncan's murder, both before and after the deed. Throughout the play, give instances of his poetic description of feelings and situations and her prosaic, practical way of thinking and expressing herself.

3. Compare Malcolm, the rightful king, with Macbeth. What motivates each of them? Does Malcolm care about his people? Does Macbeth? Compare the way Macbeth manipulates the two murderers for his own purposes and the way Malcolm temporarily deceives Macduff for the good of their country.

4. How does Shakespeare establish that Macduff is a good man? Show how Macduff's character is revealed through his actions and reactions. Focus on how he handles himself after Duncan's murder and after hearing that his wife and children have been killed.

5. Does Macbeth's character determine his fate? How does Macbeth's nature make him a prime target for the witches' temptations? Why does he choose to ignore the inner voices that tell him not to murder Duncan?

6. Is Macbeth a good man at the beginning of the play, or is he already plotting to be king? Macbeth's quick response to the suggestion that he will be king could be interpreted as proof that he has already been plotting, or it could simply show that the forces of evil have been clever in choosing their temptation. Using Macbeth's soliloquies and his scenes with Lady Macbeth, take a stand on the question and defend it.

7. Would Macbeth have murdered Duncan without Lady Macbeth's influence? The discussion will be a matter of opinion, of course. Use the scenes between Macbeth and his wife to develop and defend your view.

Motifs

1. How does the imagery of light and darkness work through the play? List instances of characters calling upon darkness to hide their evil deeds. Through light–dark imagery, trace the contest between good and evil.

2. Trace the theme of honor and loyalty throughout the play. Show how "noble Macbeth" betrays the trust placed in him, and what the consequences are. Discuss why references to loyalty and honor disappear in the middle of the play and come back at the end.

3. Fate and destiny: what is man's proper relation to them? Explore what the play is saying about this question by dividing the characters into two groups—those who trust their fate to a higher power, and those who take destiny into their own hands. Which group fares better?

4. How does the imagery relating to time work in the play? Show how Macbeth tries to compress time. Contrast his effort to "jump the life to come" with the way the honest characters let things happen as nature intends for them, in their own time.

Other Elements

1. How does the setting contribute to the play? Describe the settings of the various scenes. Show how the text indicates where a scene takes place. Discuss how the imagery of light and darkness is reflected in the setting.

2. How does the fact that *Macbeth* is one of Shakespeare's shortest plays contribute to its effectiveness? Discuss the economy of the writing. Show how each detail contributes to the advancement of the plot; and how Macbeth seems to plunge to his destruction at a sickening pace.

3. Discuss the use of dramatic tension in *Macbeth*. Chart what Shakespeare lets us know and what information he withholds from us in order to maintain suspense.

4. Social structure: How is the Scottish society of Macbeth's time ordered? How is peace maintained? Evaluate how Macbeth affects the social structure and what happens to it after Malcolm takes over.

Further Reading

CRITICAL WORKS

Bartholomeusz, Dennis. *Macbeth and the Players.* London: Cambridge University Press, 1969. This contains much historical material.

Berman, Ronald. *A Reader's Guide to Shakespeare's Plays.* Glenview, Illinois: Scott, Foresman, 1973. A bibliography and overview of critical viewpoints.

Bradley, A.C. *Shakespearean Tragedy.* New York: St. Martin's Press, 1964. A good summary of nineteenth-century criticism.

Byrne, M. St. Clare. *Elizabethan Life in Town and Country.* London: Methuen, 1954.

Charlton, H.B. *Shakespearean Tragedy.* Cambridge, England: Cambridge University Press, 1948.

Curry, Walter Clyde. *Shakespeare's Philosophical Patterns.* Binghamton, N.Y.: Vail-Ballou Press, 1937. Applies Renaissance concepts to theology and demonology to *Macbeth.*

Eliot, George Ray. *Dramatic Providence in Macbeth.* Princeton, N.J.: Princeton University Press, 1958. Includes a detailed, scene-by-scene study.

Foakes, R.A. "Suggestions for a New Approach to Shakespeare's Imagery," in *Shakespeare Survey, 5* (1952).

Hazlitt, William. *Characters of Shakespeare's Plays.* London: Oxford University Press, 1970. A classic study of Shakespeare, first published in 1817.

Knight, G. Wilson. *The Shakespearean Tempest.* London: Methuen, 1953.

Knight, G. Wilson. *The Wheel of Fire.* London: Oxford University Press, 1930.

Knights, L.C. "How Many Children Had Lady Macbeth?" in *Explorations.* England: Penguin, 1964. This classic essay treats the play as poetry, rather than as a story about people.

Murry, John Middleton. *Shakespeare.* London: Jonathan Cape, 1961.

Paul, Henry, N. *The Royal Play of Macbeth.* New York: Macmillan, 1950. Examines the influence of King James I on *Macbeth.*

Raysor, Thomas M., ed. *Coleridge's Shakespearean Criticism.* Cambridge, Mass: Harvard University Press, 1959. Criticism by poet Samuel Taylor Coleridge.

Stoll, E.E. *Art and Artifice in Shakespeare.* New York: Cambridge University Press, 1933.

Tillyard, E.M.W. *The Elizabethan World Picture.* New York: Macmillan, 1948.

Wain, John, ed. *Shakespeare: Macbeth: A Casebook.* London: Macmillan, 1968. A collection of eighteenth- and nineteenth-century criticism.

Wilson, John Dover. "Introduction," *Macbeth.* New York: Cambridge University Press, 1947.

Wright, Louis B. and LaMar, Virginia A. *The Folger Guide to Shakespeare.* New York: Washington Square Press, 1969.

AUTHOR'S OTHER WORKS

Shakespeare wrote 37 plays (38 if you include *The Two Noble Kinsmen*) over a 20-year period, from about 1590 to 1610. It's difficult to determine the exact dates when many were written, but scholars have made the following intelligent guesses about his plays and poems:

Plays

1588–93	*The Comedy of Errors*
1588–94	*Love's Labor's Lost*
1590–91	*2 Henry VI*
1590–91	*3 Henry VI*
1591–92	*1 Henry VI*
1592–93	*Richard III*
1592–94	*Titus Andronicus*

1593–94	*The Taming of the Shrew*
1593–95	*The Two Gentlemen of Verona*
1594–96	*Romeo and Juliet*
1595	*Richard II*
1594–96	*A Midsummer Night's Dream*
1596–97	*King John*
1596–97	*The Merchant of Venice*
1597	*1 Henry IV*
1597–98	*2 Henry IV*
1598–1600	*Much Ado About Nothing*
1598–99	*Henry V*
1599	*Julius Caesar*
1599–1600	*As You Like It*
1599–1600	*Twelfth Night*
1600–01	*Hamlet*
1597–1601	*The Merry Wives of Windsor*
1601–02	*Troilus and Cressida*
1602–04	*All's Well That Ends Well*
1603–04	*Othello*
1604	*Measure for Measure*
1605–06	*King Lear*
1606–07	*Antony and Cleopatra*
1605–08	*Timon of Athens*
1607–09	*Coriolanus*
1608–09	*Pericles*
1609–10	*Cymbeline*
1610–11	*The Winter's Tale*
1611–12	*The Tempest*
1612–13	*Henry VIII*

Poems

1592	*Venus and Adonis*
1593–94	*The Rape of Lucrece*
1593–1600	*Sonnets*
1600–01	*The Phoenix and the Turtle*

Glossary

Alarum Trumpet call

Augurs Prophesies

Bellona Goddess of War

Benison Blessing

Charnel Houses Bone-storage vaults

Equivocator Liar

Golgotha Place of the Skull, in Hebrew; the hill near Jerusalem where Christ was crucified, hence a place of torture or martyrdom

Gorgon A mythical female monster who was so hideous that anyone who looked at her turned to stone

Graymalkin A witch's familiar (a gray cat)

Hecate Goddess of Sorcery

Second Cock About three in the morning

Sennet Trumpet call

Tarquin Roman tyrant who raped Lucrece

Thanes Scottish noblemen

Wassail Carousing

Weird Sisters *Wyrd,* Old English for "fate"; possibly the three Fates, or Destinies

The Critics

On Lady Macbeth

The magnitude of her resolution almost covers the magnitude of her guilt. She is a great bad woman, whom we hate, but whom we fear more than we hate. . . . She is only wicked to gain a great end; and is perhaps more distinguished by her commanding presence of mind and inexorable self-will, which do not suffer her to be diverted from a bad purpose, when once formed, by weak and womanly regrets, than by the hardness of her heart or want of natural affections.

—William Hazlitt, *Characters of Shakespeare's Plays*, 1817

On Macbeth

Macbeth himself appears driven along by the violence of his fate like a vessel driven along before a storm: he reels to and fro like a drunken man; he staggers under the weight of his own purposes and the suggestions of others; he stands at bay with his situation; and from the superstitious awe and breathless suspense into which the communications of the Weird Sisters throw him, is hurried on with daring impatience to verify their predictions, and with impious and bloody hand to tear aside the veil which hides the uncertainty of the future.

—William Hazlitt, *Characters of Shakespeare's Plays*, 1817

On Macbeth's Morality

Macbeth remains an honorable gentleman. He is not a criminal; he has no criminal tendencies. But once permit his self-love to demand a satisfaction which cannot be honestly attained, and he is likely to grasp any dishonorable means to that end which may be safely employed. In other words, Macbeth has much of the *natural* good in him unimpaired; environment has conspired with his nature to make him upright in all his dealings with those about him. But *moral* goodness in him is undeveloped and indeed still rudimentary, for his voluntary acts are scarcely brought into harmony with ultimate ends.

—Walter Clyde Curry, *Shakespeare's Philosophical Patterns,* 1937

On the Imagery of Darkness

Darkness, we may even say blackness, broods over this tragedy. It is remarkable that almost all the scenes which at once recur to memory take place either at night or in some dark spot. The vision of the dagger, the murder of Duncan, the sleep-walking of Lady Macbeth, all come in night-scenes. The Witches dance in the thick air of a storm, or "black and midnight hags" receive Macbeth in a cavern. The blackness of night is to the hero a thing of fear, even of horror; and that which he feels becomes the spirit of the play.

—A.C. Bradley, *Shakespearean Tragedy.* 1964

On the Imagery in Macbeth

The play opens with thunder and the appearance of the witches, and a succession of immediate and effective visual or auditory images is presented directly to an audience or imaginative reader by means of the bleeding sergeant, the bloody daggers and hands, the knocking at the gate, the banquet with the ghost of Banquo, the apparitions, and the sleep-walking. These effects establish the play's atmosphere, and form a kind of framework to the poetic imagery.

—R.A. Foakes, "Suggestions for a New Approach to Shakespeare's Imagery." 1952

On Lady Macbeth

Lady Macbeth, like all in Shakespeare, is a class individualized:—of high rank, left much alone, and feeding herself with day-dreams of ambition, she mistakes the courage of fantasy for the power of bearing the consequences of the realities of guilt. Hers is the mock fortitude of a mind deluded by ambition; she shames her husband with a superhuman audacity of fancy which she cannot support, but sinks in the season of remorse, and dies in suicidal agony.

—Samuel Taylor Coleridge, *Coleridge's Shakespearean Criticism;* edited by Thomas M. Raysor, 1959